## Praise for *She Appears! Encounters with Kwan Yin, Goddess o*

C000102811

A great and moving chorus of voices. We urgently need this book to bring Kwan
sionate and fierce energy into all our lives.

> — **Susan Griffin,** author of *Wrestling with the Angel of Democracy:*
> *On Being an American Citizen.*

This unusual book is a vivid testimonial to the appeal the East Asian Buddhist "goddess" Kwan Yin holds
for Westerners. These first person accounts of how Kwan Yin entered peoples' lives and the art work
and poetry about her that they produced are unique among accounts of Western Buddhist practice. Both
scholars of Buddhism and Buddhist practitioners will find these accounts relevant for different reasons.
For scholars, they provide contemporary and culturally familiar accounts of how this much loved East
Asian goddess can impact peoples' lives here and now. For practitioners, they provide immediate inspiration for further devotion to this goddess from the East who, nevertheless, enters the lives of Westerners.

> — **Rita M. Gross,** author of *Buddhism after Patriarchy: A Feminist History,*
> *Analysis, and Reconstruction of Buddhism* and Buddhist teacher

She Appears! Is a beautiful book created by Sandy Boucher that tells first-hand experiences of women to
whom Kwan Yin appeared. Kwan Yin came in many forms: as deep compassion, healing energy, unconditional mother love, usually at times of crisis. She is often a felt presence and is also seen as an image. She
is an archetype (that I described in Goddesses in Older Women), an Asian goddess, and a bodhisattva in
Buddhism. In words, paintings, drawings, and sculpture, contributors tell their experience of She-who-
hears-the-cries-of –the-world. To all who ask, Kwan Yin pours out mercy and gives comfort. No one has
to be somehow deserving. The great value of this book is that it serves as an introduction to a source that
anyone can call upon.

> — **Jean Shinoda Bolen, M.D.** author of *Artemis: the Indomitable Spirit in Everywoman*

In the beauty of this book I find both solace and inspiration. Its tapestry of word and imagery evokes a
rapt and open stillness that feels close to the core of true compassion. Praise be for the nourishment of
soul and senses that Sandy Boucher brings us in this global moment.

> — **Joanna Macy,** author of *Coming Back to Life:*
> *The Updated Guide to the Work That Reconnects*

This is the kind of book you can open to any page and, in just a few moments, feel its supportive gifts. In this book Sandy has gathered and shared the beauty, richness and power of Kwan Yin's influence in the West.

— **Sharon Salzberg,** Co-Founder of The Insight Meditation Society
and author of *Real Happiness: The Power of Meditation*

This book beautifully demonstrates the living presence of Kwan Yin in our midst. The weave of personal accounts and art form an inspiring spiritual gift.

— **Charlene Spretnak,** author of *Lost Goddesses of Early Greece:
A Collection of Pre-Hellenic Myths*

Sandy Boucher has created a splendid tapestry of stories, memories, dreams and images of Kwan Yin in her new book, She Appears! Along with a rich mix of her own beautifully crafted vignettes and memoirs, she has interspersed dozens of offerings from other devotees of this Chinese Savior Goddess. The writings are touching and the artwork exquisite, facilitating a visceral contact with the Asian Great Goddess of Compassion. Poignant and inspiring.

— **Vicki Noble,** healer, writer, artist and teacher, co-creator of Motherpeace and author of *Shakti Woman: Feeling our Fire, Healing our World* and *The Double Goddess: Women Sharing Power*

On retreat with my mother, she awoke early on the morning she was due to receive the initiation to find White Tara standing beside her holding a lotus which she gave to my mother as she dissolved into light. Later a Lama remarked "Well, everyone gets to see Tara."

One can speak of psychological projections, but the fact is that she appears! As Tara, Kwan Yin or the Virgin Mary, the divine feminine is very close to us and ready to help whenever possible. Her compassionate assistance is tangible like a mother with her child. Appearing in many forms and guises the divine feminine is there for all of us if we would only reach out to Her.

This book of personal accounts, poems and artwork devoted to Kwan Yin by a variety of practitioners, exemplifies the wide range of Kwan Yin's activities and will hopefully introduce this great Bodhisattva to a wider audience. We are grateful to Sandy Boucher for compiling this collection of inspiring anecdotes and paintings.

— **Tenzin Palmo,** author of *Reflections on a Mountain Lake: Teachings on
Practical Buddhism* and celebrated in the book by Vicki Mackenzie
*Cave in the Snow: Tenzin Palmo's Quest for Enlightenment*

This deeply inspiring volume is made up of numerous experiences of Kwan Yin, Goddess of Compassion, both experiences of the main author, Sandy Boucher, well known Buddhist writer and teacher, and of her numerous friends and correspondents who sent her their poems, accounts and images of their experience of the Goddess. These experiences flow across many moments in life, experiences of nature, of family relationships, of healing and peace in times of distress and hopelessness, in struggles against injustices, and times of sickness and death. These are times of "precious revelations" when we experience the "responsiveness of the universe" in the appearances of Kwan Yin in our lives. This is a book to keep near at hand, to read and reread, to tap into for the deep moments of love, peace and renewed wellbeing.

— **Rosemary Radford Ruether,** theologian and author of
*Sexism and God Talk: Toward a Feminist Theology*

Kwan Yin invites personal relationships, creates indelible memories, harvests compassion, and evokes power. Sandy Boucher captures all of it and more in an exquisite volume. Treat yourself to the amazing images. Embrace the poignant prose.

Let Kwan Yin's eyes invite your own connection to her. This is feminist spirituality lived in community, loved into action.

— **Mary E. Hunt,** Co-director, Women's Alliance for Theology, Ethics and Ritual, (WATER)
and co-editor with Diann L. Neu of *New Feminist Christianity: Many Voices, Many Views*

In She Appears! Encounters with Kwan Yin, Goddess of Compassion, Sandy Boucher has compiled a sumptuous feast of writing and artwork about the beloved Asian Goddess, the Celestial Bodhisattva of Compassion, Kwan Yin. Like Boucher, many—but not all—of the contributors in this volume are Buddhists—meditators, Zen priests, nuns, teachers, students. All have been profoundly touched by the very real presence of Kwan Yin in their lives and they share their personal stories through memoir and artwork.

Boucher notes that the collection was "born from the urgency of many people who expressed their desire to share their experience of powerful, in some cases life-changing connection with ... Kwan Yin." For some of the contributors, that encounter was dramatic, bringing about an epiphany. For others, Kwan Yin slowly transformed their lives in gradual yet equally profound ways. Whether you have long known and loved Kwan Yin or are newly learning about her, this book will feed your soul. It is inspiring, thought-provoking, comforting, soothing, and a clarion call to compassionate activism. The stories and artwork are imbued with an intimacy that is at once individual and universal. In a world all-too-often devoid of loving-kindness and compassion, this book reminds us that Kwan Yin is alive and well—ready to nurture and sustain us.

— **Mary Saracino,** author of *Heretics: A Love Story*

**Also by Sandy Boucher**

*Dancing in the Dharma: The Life and Teachings of Ruth Denison*

*Hidden Spring: A Buddhist Woman Confronts Cancer*

*Discovering Kwan Yin: Buddhist Goddess of Compassion*

*Opening the Lotus: A Woman's Guide to Buddhism*

*Turning the Wheel: American Women Creating the New Buddhism*

*Heartwomen: An Urban Feminist's Odyssey Home*

*The Notebooks of Leni Clare* (stories)

*Assaults & Rituals* (stories)

*Taking the Leap* by Pema Chodron (editor)

# She Appears!

## Encounters with Kwan Yin, Goddess of Compassion

By Sandy Boucher

Goddess Ink

www.goddess-ink.com

Copyright ©2015 by Sandy Boucher

All rights reserved. No part of this book may be reproduced in any form or by any electronic or mechanical means, or the facilitation thereof, including information storage and retrieval systems, without permission in writing from the publisher, except by a reviewer, who may quote brief passages in a review.

Printed in the United States of America

ISBN: 978-0-9833466-6-1

Published by

Goddess Ink
www.goddess-ink.com

Designed by Soujanya Rao

Front cover artwork by Willow B. Norris www.willowbnorris.com
Author photo by Ann Ziegler
All rights reserved, used with permission.

"Kansas City Kwan Yin," Guanyin of the Southern Sea, Chinese, Liao (907–1125) or Jin Dynasty (1115–1234). Wood with polychrome, 95 x 65 inches. The Nelson-Atkins Museum of Art, Kansas City, Missouri. Purchase: William Rockhill Nelson Trust, 34–10. Photo: Jamison Miller.

Mary B. Kelly's "Kwan Yin of Putuo Shan Island" first appeared in Kelly's book, *Goddess Women Cloth* (Studiobooks, 2011).

Miriam Davis's "I Hear Your Cries, I Come" and "Kwan Yin Takes a Break" photographed by Anita Frimkess Fein.

*For Emmie,*
*always in my heart*

# CONTENTS

## Chapter Six
## Kwan Yin as Activist

## Chapter Seven
## Death and Grieving

### Chapter Eight

# Chapter One
# Hearing the Cries of the World

*She Appears* was born from the urgency of many people who expressed their desire to share their experience of powerful, in some cases life-changing connection with the transcendent presence of the Celestial Bodhisattva of Compassion, Kwan Yin. Soon after publishing my book, *Discovering Kwan Yin*, fifteen years ago, I began to receive a flood of stories telling how Kwan Yin appeared in a time of distress and hopelessness, and how that visitation had changed a person's awareness, comforted or encouraged her, or healed her. A wealth of artwork also arrived—images of the benevolent goddess in paintings, sculptures, drawings, and prints—from powerful to whimsical, often with a mini-story attached describing the circumstances in which this particular evocation of Kwan Yin had made herself known. The offerings came primarily from the United States, but some also arrived from Canada, Australia, and South Africa. Some of these communications were highly crafted, sent by professional artists and writers; others were stories in plain language, simple images, sent by people who do not consider themselves writers or visual artists but whose stories expressed the power, wonderment, and gratitude of women and men who had benefited from their contact with Kwan Yin.

These people's writings and visual images fascinated me and made me feel I knew each sender. Some brought me to tears as I felt their suffering and their wonder at Kwan Yin's gift to them. The whimsy of some of the artwork elicited a chuckle. I kept them all. And then several years ago I realized that these messages needed to be taken out of my file drawer and given a broader life in the world. In these dangerous times, we beleaguered citizens, neighbors, and friends need the courage, comfort, and self-nurturing that allow us to act with compassion toward others. Knowing Kwan Yin offers all this, I sent out a call for more stories and images, and received a resounding response.

Surrounded by the abundance of earlier and more recent submissions, savoring my contact with the flow of compassionate, healing energy that is Kwan Yin, seeing the lovely, stunning, revelatory images of the goddess through the eyes of artists, I began to understand that this book is not a simple anthology or collection, useful as that might be, but a volume of precious revelations offering Kwan Yin's balm of total acceptance of all that is, opening a doorway into a more engaged, more passionate life.

Who is this Asian goddess who commands such a vibrant place in the lives of these Western women and men? Why and how has she found her way into the hearts of so many? Her name means "she who hears the cries of the world." She steps in to save people from danger, to comfort those in distress, to offer guidance to the confused and alienated. Kwan Yin is best known as a Buddhist emanation, but she is widely revered among goddess worshippers, former Catholics, and people needing help. She holds the title of Ascended Master in the Theosophical faith and appears in other esoteric religions. Kwan Yin seems to cross the boundaries between religious and spiritual disciplines easily, appearing in ancient traditions and New Age formulations. True to her mission, she appears when most needed to whoever may be suffering. No credentials required.

Kwan Yin—also known as Quan yin, Guan-Shih-Yin, Kannon, Kwannon, Quan Am, Kwan Seum Bosal, she of the many names—is the pre-eminent goddess in all of Asia. She is revered as a bodhisattva in China, Japan, Vietnam, Korea, and other Asian countries. The *bodhisattva* is a person who pursues her path to awakening or enlightenment but stops before final liberation, vowing, "I will not achieve full liberation until every being in the universe is enlightened." She turns back into the world, returning life after life to do everything she can to alleviate suffering and to wake people up. Kwan Yin is such a being. Called the Celestial Bodhisattva of Compassion, she expresses unconditional caring in all her actions: healing, guiding, stepping forward to pluck a drowning person from the waves, extinguishing a life-threatening fire, heading off the pirates who would attack a boatload of helpless refugees. She can take many forms, adopting the identity best suited to the circumstances: she may appear in a female or a male body, noble or humble, as a rich philanthropist, a sword-wielding general, a fishwife, the clerk in the grocery store at the corner of your street.

She is viewed by some as the great compassionate mother who comforts and supports her children; if asked, she brings a baby to the childless. But she is more often seen as the supple maiden-goddess, her robe blown by the sea wind, or as the deep meditator who sits looking inward in perfect peace. She carries a vial holding the fluid of compassion, which she pours out over the world. She rides a dragon, sometimes a lion or elephant, comfortable with the wild primal energy of these creatures. Her sword cuts through confusion to the shining jewel of truth. She stands or sits near crashing waves or placid flowing water, under a willow tree, under a moon. In her left hand she carries a long-stemmed lotus blossom, symbol of the truth that purity is rooted in the muck and mire of experience, as the lotus stem rises from the mud at the bottom of the pond up through murky water, its petals opening on the surface into the flower of perfect awareness.

## A Stunning Transformation

Kwan Yin's change from male to female in ancient China is a unique event in world religion. The male bodhisattva of compassion, Avalokiteshvara, was brought to China sometime after Buddhism was imported from India in the early centuries of the Common Era. By the eighth century, female forms of Avalokiteshvara began to appear, and by the ninth century, the female Guan Shih Yin or Kwan Yin became the dominant representation of compassion. What this change of gender may say about the ancient Chinese view of women I cannot guess, but I know that in every civilization there exists a hunger for the feminine divine. We who were born female long to see our spiritual guides embodied in female form. Buddhist tradition holds that enlightenment transcends gender, an assertion that must make sense to any thoughtful person, but still we less-than-enlightened folks are left with all the gender differences and inequities that operate in our daily lives and spiritual communities. We hunger to see femaleness mirrored in the figures that inspire us, for if I am to aspire to Buddhahood, how much better for my progress to have the model of a Buddha who shares the awareness and responses that I experience every day in my female body. And if I were a man, I might be relieved to see a female Buddha and grateful to view the Buddhist path more inclusively.

Deborah Bowman, author of *The Female Buddha*, says, "In celebrating an image of the female Buddha, we challenge the old myth with a new myth. We play with form to shake up habitual thinking and honor diverse paths to [liberation]." And she adds, "The female Buddha points to a shifting paradigm beyond prejudice, asking us to step forward and bring freedom to all."

## Many Forms, One Compassionate Energy

The writers and artists you will meet in the following pages bring Kwan Yin to resonant life. Their stories and artwork, gathered here, come from their hearts, in acknowledgment of the deep healing power of Kwan Yin's spirit and image. The features of the goddess in some of these drawings, sculptures, and paintings will seem more Caucasian than Asian. Of course, many citizens of the West have Asian features and backgrounds and see themselves mirrored in the more traditional Chinese, Japanese, Korean, or Vietnamese depictions of Kwan Yin, but those of us of other ethnic backgrounds experience her with our own bodies and minds, see ourselves in her, and may visualize her as looking more like us. The vast compassionate energy of Kwan Yin is not bound by any nationality or ethnic group.

In dreams and waking visions, Kwan Yin answers the cries of suffering; she arrives at the foot of a hospital bed to offer reassurance, or to teach a set of therapeutic movements. In answer to the anguish of psychological struggle and despondency, she appears as a small figure perched on the corner of a shower stall, to offer guidance. Mothers, widowed or facing the dissolution of their marriage, afraid for themselves and their children, tell of Kwan Yin coming in a dream to speak to them, to communicate that "All will be well." Certainly, some of the images express joy and humor, such as the whimsical sculpture, "Kwan Yin Takes a Break," or the depiction of Kwan Yin accompanied by a small, delighted child, riding on the back of a bear. In the East and the West, Kwan Yin offers unconditional compassion for all beings. And she can be present in the dying process, to ease the transition, and give succor to those who grieve.

One of the first people to write to me after I published *Discovering Kwan Yin* was a woman in her late fifties named Mary Cutsinger. Mother and artist, she lived with her husband in a small town in the Mojave Desert in California, where he had worked at the nearby airbase. Mary sent me her story of encountering Kwan Yin. Her first husband had died at an early age, after which she found herself alone with their five small daughters, and it was then she received Kwan Yin's blessing. She sent me a painting she had done at that time of the bodhisattva with a tear showing on her cheek, for Kwan Yin had helped Mary understand that, while she had to stay strong to support her children in their loss, she must also allow herself to experience her own grief. Mary became my friend, and invited my partner and me to her desert community to lead meditation retreats. She sent me other paintings of Kwan Yin, and gave me a print of her large crying Kwan Yin. Then she fell ill with cancer, diagnosed too late. She died at age 77, after months of suffering. But Mary's energy continues to inform my own awareness of Kwan Yin's presence in our lives; you will meet her and see her paintings in this book.

While I have learned much about Kwan Yin from reading scholarly studies about the bodhisattva and from my own experiences with her, the women and men who have entrusted their stories to me have drawn me further into the life blood of Kwan Yin's coming to the West. They have taken me vividly into nature, where she dwells, depicting her as a green Oregon mountain, writing about the role of a tree in bringing a mother and daughter together, showing her in water, her natural element, peeking out from behind the curve of a hill, or hovering tenderly over a bare desert landscape.

They have shown me how Kwan Yin can intercede or be present in difficult encounters where political/cultural poisons threaten, such as with Tibetan women in China, an Arab bride in Jaffa, or a menacing bigot in Oregon. One concerned person sent me a Kwan Yin prayer for victims of abuse. These stories illustrate my own experience that Kwan Yin's sword cuts through confusion and can allow us to perform the radical maneuver of leading with the heart—leading with love.

The artists have found truly original ways to render Kwan Yin, portraying her as their artistic and spiritual vision dictates. And several have combined her with the feminine divine from other traditions, as in the "Pele-Kwanyin" painting that joins her with the great Hawaiian goddess Pele; or Kwan Yin bearing the image of the ancient mother goddess, called the Venus of Laussel, in her headdress; or, more commonly, merged with the Christian Virgin Mary. Whether in a simple painting on cardboard or an elegantly produced computer image, each piece of art delivers a unique experience and vision.

Of course, Kwan Yin is amply and sometimes bewilderingly present on the Internet. Google her and you'll find everything from the websites of acupuncture/herb practitioners to channeled messages; from art-for-sale to descriptions of Kwan Yin as an Ascended Master; from YouTube guided meditations and ritual dances evoking Kwan Yin to divination cards and even a game or two, just to name a few highlights. Some of this entertains, some of it informs or enlightens, some of it causes me to cringe. But having acknowledged this wealth of information, which ranges from excellent to embarrassing, I have not included any further examples in this book. Anyone who wants to spend some time surfing the net will find a great array of information and many gems.

Since my first engagement with Kwan Yin so many years ago, I have become more intimate with illness and death; this has made me more willing to be present with the discomfort and occasional pain of my existence, to open to others in distress, and to surrender more wholeheartedly to the joy that comes with connection. My experience teaches that extreme suffering, watched over and comforted by Kwan Yin, can inspire the recipient to turn the gift around, to offer a similar comfort to those in pain. This phenomenon comes alive in the stories in this book, some of them my own.

I hope this book will find its way to the sickroom, the hospital room, the kitchen and workroom and back porch, the lonely 3 a.m. bedroom, for these authors and artists illustrate the truth that Kwan Yin appears most radiantly in the darkest of human situations. She is not some remote elusive figure but is accessible to us in every moment, every situation. She is the deepest, most authentic part of ourselves, always responsive if called upon sincerely. A Buddhist-teacher friend asks her students to go about their day seeing themselves as Kwan Yin and recognizing Kwan Yin in others. At first they think they are pretending to be Kwan Yin, but soon they see themselves as Kwan Yin pretending to be their ordinary selves. That brings home the truth of her presence in each of our hearts.

May the following stories and artwork reach out to touch you, wake you up to your own aliveness, so you can shed the tears you need to shed, marvel at the episodes brought to vibrant life here, perhaps see yourself in some of them, let out a throaty chuckle or a full laugh from deep in your belly, and feel Kwan Yin's love for yourself and all beings.

## Kwan Yin – Poem by Laura Fargas

Laura Fargas offers a unique perspective in this poem. Bypassing the often exalted depictions of Kwan Yin, she situates the young bodhisattva firmly in everyday life.

Of the many buddhas I love best the girl
who will not leave the cycle of pain before anyone else.
It is not the captain declining to be saved
on the sinking ship, who may just want to ride his shame
out of sight. She is at the brink of never being hurt again
but pauses to say, All of us. Every blade of grass.
She chooses to live in the tumble of souls through time.
Perhaps she sees spring in every country,
talks quietly with farm women while helping to lay seed.
Our hearts are a storm she trembles at. I picture her
leaning on a tree or humming or joining a volleyball game
on Santa Monica beach. Her skin shines with sweat.

The others may not know how to notice what she does to them.
She is not a fish or a bee; it is not pity or thirst;
she could go, but here she is.

## How Kwan Yin Found Me: A Tale of Resistance and Surrender
## – Memoir by Sandy Boucher
## Sculpture by 12th century Chinese artist

Just so you understand, I was not a goddess person. You wouldn't have caught me in a long flowered peasant skirt, and it was only very occasionally that I joined a circle of ecstatic women to dance under the full moon. No, I was a feet-on-the-ground political activist and writer, exclusively committed to this-world experience and skeptical of anything even faintly redolent of spirituality or religion. When, back in the seventies, I heard some of my feminist friends begin to talk about the Great Goddess or wax lyrical about our matriarchal heritage, I thought they had slipped their moorings and drifted out into Lalaland.

So, imagine my surprise: It's 1982. I'm in Kansas City on my way east and I find myself in a giant room in an art gallery. This is the Nelson Atkins Museum of Asian Art. Looking down at me is a female figure, richly dressed, with Asian features. She is eight feet high, seated with one knee up, one arm balanced on her raised knee.

I would never have found my own way here, skeptical as I was about the whole subject of goddesses, but an acquaintance brought me to this room, perhaps because she knew I had begun to practice Buddhist meditation and this statue had something to do with Buddhism. She brought me before this majestic, exquisitely beautiful sculpture, said, "This is Kwan Yin" (a name I had never heard before) and left me alone with the goddess.

Oops, I thought. I'm losing my bearings. I have no context for this figure, no guide to orient me.

**"Kansas City Kwan Yin,"** Guanyin of the Southern Sea, Chinese, Liao (907–1125) or Jin Dynasty (1115–1234).
Wood with polychrome, 95 x 65 inches. The Nelson-Atkins Museum of Art, Kansas City, Missouri.
Purchase: William Rockhill Nelson Trust, 34-10. Photo: Jamison Miller.

# She Appears!

Alone in the room, I stood looking up into Kwan Yin's face. Her body contained something tremendously powerful. It radiated up from her commanding posture as she sat on a piece of rock, one foot up, the other on a lotus blossom. The label at the base of the statue informed me that she was carved of wood, then painted, sometime between the 10th and 13th centuries in China.

So how could this piece of wood, sculpted hundreds of years ago, be so fully alive? How could it embody something ineffable, something not measurable, something others would call "spirit"? These questions nagged at me but, as I gazed up at her, not able to turn away or leave the room, I felt the hard edges of my resistance begin to soften. Whatever it is that resides in Kwan Yin reached out to pierce my tight container, and I felt my boundaries fluttering, giving way, to allow something hidden and unexplored to rise up in me. It was as if I was held in a cone of thick, slowly fluctuating energy that came from her but also from somewhere inside myself.

"Kwan Yin," I said to myself, trying out the words. "So, is this a goddess?"

It was a time in my life when I was struggling to find some balance, having been focused resolutely outward for a decade. In the seventies, I had given myself wholeheartedly to the efforts of the Women's Liberation Movement to bring equal rights and full recognition to women. Leaving the safety of marriage and a clerical job, I had helped bring together a collective of women and children and one man. We lived together in a house in San Francisco, published a newspaper called *Mother Lode*, and planned and led demonstrations against businesses and organizations that excluded or oppressed women. We provided safe haven for women fleeing abusive boyfriends or husbands, and free temporary lodging for activists new in town; and we alternated childcare duties, living our belief that children were not private property but beings whose care should be shared by all. This was a passionate, 24-hour-a-day commitment in which I felt hugely alive and useful in the world. I felt I was making revolutionary change in a wholesome direction.

After the collective broke up, I continued to engage in political activism with other groups and projects. But gradually I came to recognize the price of this lifestyle, realizing I had no idea how to take care of myself, either physically or spiritually. I didn't know how to replenish the energy I was constantly sending outward, and so I was often sick or seriously exhausted. I knew how to write a leaflet, participate in a sidewalk demonstration, organize protection for a woman whose boyfriend had shot the lock off her door, or stay up all night writing an article responding to an abusive newspaper piece. But I did not know how to nourish myself by touching a deeper reality that might sustain me.

Then, in 1980, with a lover, I found my way to Buddhist practice and began to meditate regularly.

Soon, I felt myself beginning to open to a calmer, more inward mode of being. But I adamantly resisted any pull toward the supernatural or the sacred, and refused to entertain the possibility of realities other than this material world I inhabited.

This was my condition when I found myself standing before the statue of Kwan Yin. When I left the museum that day, I took her with me in the form of a postcard of the statue, for I could not deny my experience. Certainly it was improbable, definitely not part of my repertory, yet I deeply felt the reality of that half hour with Kwan Yin's energy. Something had shifted inside me; a door had opened.

This was the beginning of the spiritual path I have followed ever since.

One of the contributors to this book reports that she used to view Kwan Yin's presence and powers as "comforting myths," until she had a direct experience herself. But what is a myth? Bronislav Malinowsky, the Polish anthropologist, defines it as "the re-arising of primordial reality in story form." In the decades since that day in Kansas City, I have taken the trouble to inform myself about the primordial reality of matriarchy and the Goddess, looking at the archeological evidence, particularly the ancient statues of female figures obviously born of and intended for veneration (cf. Marija Gimbutas, Vicki Noble, et al.). Gradually, my vision has expanded to include the documentation of the foundation of female agency and power, and the present-day immanence of the figures we call the Divine Feminine. Does that make me a goddess person? You bet. My mind and heart are now open to the towering emanations of female spiritual agency from many cultures and religions. I celebrate matriarchal energy wherever I find it.

Much of my personal exploration of Kwan Yin has centered on the quality of compassion that she embodies: how it is expressed in my life, or not expressed. In the retreats I lead, held in Kwan Yin's embrace, we write about our experiences of giving compassion, of receiving it, and of not being able to give or receive. In my personal life with my partner, family, and community, I am continually challenged to act from my essential caring self rather than react with conditioned patterns of fear, judgment, or self-protectiveness that cause such pain.

The example of Kwan Yin bodhisattva always offers me a deeper, more authentic alternative to my careless or programmed behavior, or to ill-considered or wrongly motivated acts of compassion. She holds all of us to a purer standard.

Over the years, I have called upon Kwan Yin in settings of extreme illness, political conflict, and everyday joys and sorrows. I am unendingly fascinated by her many embodiments and visitations. In this book, I open to the wisdom and heart of a community of women and men who bring their intelligence and perception to their experience of the Bodhisattva of Compassion. This is a natural development of spiritual journey: first seeking inward for Kwan Yin's presence, succor, and significance, over decades and in many situations; and later, now, opening out to embrace and to learn from my sisters and brothers, who are likewise open to Kwan Yin's example, and who help me recognize that we are not separate.

In a way, the gathering of material for this book mirrors my first encounter with Kwan Yin in Kansas City. Reading the words of others, admiring the images others have created, affects me in much the same way as I was affected during that first half-hour in Kwan Yin's presence. Now, so many years later, I feel a further softening of my rigidities, a surrender of long-held boundaries. Weaving these expressions together, I walk a path of changing perspective and deepening peace. I invite you, reader, to enter into the experiences evoked in the following pages with your eyes and mind and heart open. It's Kwan Yin's voice you'll hear, Kwan Yin's eyes you'll look through.

# Chapter Two
# Alive in Nature

When I hike in the woods on the ridge above Oakland, I sense how strongly Kwan Yin exists around me. Looking ahead down the dirt path where it bends to disappear among the rough trunks of redwoods, the dusty foliage of oaks, sometimes I imagine that I will glimpse her there at the edge of the trail, standing back among the shrubbery, calmly watching. Farther down the path I come upon a burned stump, waist-high, which from a distance bears the contours of a seated Kwan Yin, legs folded, back subtly curved, head tipped slightly down in meditation posture. This always makes me smile, seeing her so clearly outlined, sitting there blessing all who pass. And I trust that the other hikers are touched by her benevolent presence as they stride by.

Just as the indigenous people of this country teach us that every element of the natural world is a conscious, alive, and responsive being, letting us know we are only one strand in the great weave of life's unfolding, so Kwan Yin signals a similar awareness. She is always shown outside—at the seashore or riding on tumultuous ocean waves, next to still or running water, under a willow tree, or with a full moon above her. These settings announce that she is one with all creatures, she is part of nature.

It was in the forests of India that the Buddha sat down under a tree to meditate and seek enlightenment. When, just before his liberation, the forces of evil threatened him, he reached down to touch the earth, going to that primal foundation, the mother of us all, for protection. Like the Buddha, Kwan Yin shares the energy of the trees and the rocks and the water.

We know that our own bodies are composed of the physical elements of earth, water, fire, and air, and utterly dependent upon them. Our indigenous sisters remind us that we are related to everything in nature, and that the air and water, trees, animals, fish, and fowl need our attention. Kwan Yin is not separate from the elements, nor indifferent to the destruction of the natural environment in our contemporary world. She invites us to enter deeply into intimacy with all beings.

In a traditional Buddhist guided meditation, Kwan Yin descends from the full moon to stand in the shining path of moonlight on the ocean waves. Then she comes forward to enter us, to open our hearts to ourselves and to all beings. In this process, she teaches us to nurture ourselves, but then she opens our compassion to all creatures, asking us to act from our healed and strengthened selves, to move out and heal the creatures of the earth. She wants us to feel our affinity with all living things and to understand that what we do to the earth and its creatures is what we do to ourselves.

# On Kwan Yin's Sacred Island – Memoir by Sandy Boucher

My own first strong awareness of Kwan Yin in the natural world came on the beach of an island in the South China Sea. The tiny island, called Putuo Shan (holy mountain), is dedicated to Kwan Yin. It has been a pilgrimage site for hundreds of years, a place people come to visit the many temples and sea caves, hoping to receive the bodhisattva's blessing, and even to have a vision of her.

I journeyed to this distant site with a Chinese-American friend who is devoted to Kwan Yin. We hoped to feel her presence strongly in a way that was not possible in the West. After all, China is Kwan Yin's first home, and she must be rooted powerfully there, we thought. We even imagined, in typical pilgrim fashion, that she would show herself to us in a vision. Now I wonder whether my urgency to come to this island had been fueled by an unconscious need to prepare for what awaited me back in the United States. I could not have known then that in a few months I would be diagnosed with third-stage cancer, undergo major surgery, and begin a long, debilitating course of chemotherapy, or that I would draw upon my experience on Putuo Shan to meet the daily emergency of serious illness.

After six days of visiting the sites on the humid hills of the little island, I was frustrated. At every temple large groups of Asian tourists stampeded through, often led by a guide shouting into a bullhorn. Our hope of meditating in the temples with the magnificent Kwan Yin statues was dashed when we found they were run like museums, with ropes preventing us from entering and monk-guards watching to make sure we did not trespass. Most of the tourists had come to sunbathe on the long flat beaches, swim in the sea, and eat in the fish restaurants along the shore. Only a few sincere pilgrims joined us in offering incense at the temples.

I wanted closer contact with Kwan Yin, some sign that she really did reside here on her "holy mountain." So I awoke at 5:30 a.m. in our hotel room and, leaving my friend asleep, I went out to walk to the beach, intuiting that I would find her at the water's edge.

The shore swept down the long curve of a bay, new light from the eastern horizon barely touching the sand, restless waves stirring the brownish surf. Breathing deeply of the sea air, I went down to the sand, cool under my bare feet, and started my hike all the way to the end of the beach. There I found a shelf of rock that was backed by bushes, which would shade me from the sun's violence when it rose high in the sky. I sat down, noting the lovely sweep of pale-sand shore and sky filling with dawn light. I looked up the beach to Chaoyin Cave, the first place we had visited on the island, and saw that the few people who had already come out were still far away. I would be alone here for a long time. Finding a flat place on the rock, I sat down cross-legged, closed my eyes, and settled inward.

Just to make sure she knew I was there, I intoned the words "Namo Guan Shih Yin Pusa." ("I call upon you, Kwan Yin Bodhisattva," or "I take refuge in you, Kwan Yin Bodhisattva.") I had learned this chant at a Chinese monastery in California; now it felt right to bring it back to its first home and use it to announce my presence here. "Namo Guan Shih Yin Pusa" ("Hey, Kwan Yin, here I am!") Then I fell silent.

Cicadas buzzed loudly in the bushes behind me; to my left the waves murmured as they pushed up onto the sand. The breeze gently touched me, keeping me cool. Gradually, I began to experience each of these as the voice and presence of Kwan Yin. The rock was Kwan Yin, too, and the big brown bugs skittering about, and my own body/mind process as I sat there, all expressed Kwan Yin. My awareness of her manifested in an utterly physical way, a knowledge felt in my cells, my blood, and my lymph, and it was deeply reassuring. This body that, still unbeknownst to me, carried a deadly cancer, was telling me, Yes, she will hear your cry. Yes, she inhabits every part of you, even the malignant cells in your gut.

The few people down the beach kept their distance. Now and then I opened my eyes to slap the rock and startle the big bugs away, preventing them from crawling into my bag or up my pant legs. Very shy, they skittered off. I settled fully into the elements—ocean, rock, breeze, heat of sun—knowing them all to be Kwan Yin; that is to say, the spirit inherent in all the elements and their motion. I stayed a long time, sitting, until the sun rode its way up the sky and devoured the protective shade of the shrub behind me.

When I made my way back to the hotel room, I found Kwan Yin in the tree outside in the courtyard, in a bird chirping, flowing reflections of light from the surface of the pool up onto the beams of the hotel; I found her on the table cluttered with chopsticks, the small red biscuit package, the plastic bag of almonds; she was in my hand holding the pen and moving across the pale lavender page of my journal, and in the ticking of the vent through which cool air flowed into the room. My thoughts anchored me in the great web of consciousness that is China, the world. My body was comfortable for the moment, at ease, a container for the thread of my human awareness. All this spoke Kwan Yin.

## Kwan Yin of Putuo Shan Island – Painting by Mary B. Kelly

Mary B. Kelly, who herself visited Putuo Shan, created an image evoking the bodhisattva's expansive presence on that sacred island. Kelly, an artist, art professor, and author, lives and works in South Carolina. Her painting shows a towering figure of Kwan Yin pouring out the waters of compassion with one hand while holding, in her other hand, a willow branch to sprinkle dew on the land.

When I saw this painting, I immediately recognized the quality of my own experience on Putuo Shan. Here we see Kwan Yin in a sea-green robe, standing on the back of a fish in the water, near the island, three pilgrimage mountains behind her on the mainland. Lotuses adorn her headdress and bodice, and a lotus mandala opens behind her head.

**Kwan Yin of Putuo Shan Island,**
Mary B. Kelly

# Kwan Yin Appears – Memoir by Musawa

Far from the roiling waters of the South China Sea, along the northern coast of the United States, Kwan Yin appeared from among the trees and worked her magic on a woman whose life is deeply joined with nature. Musawa is one of the earliest pioneers of the women's land movement in Oregon, in which women bought land and learned to farm it, built houses and created communities, some of which still exist. She has dedicated her life to living sustainably in the woods, teaching others to respect and nurture the natural world. She was a founding editor of *We'Moon*, the lunar calendar datebook that she and her collective still publish after three decades. For many years, Musawa earned her living as a healer, offering bodywork. The stunning encounter she describes, seemingly an initiation, is related to her training in helping people heal body and mind.

Musawa writes:

*I am sitting in the woods on our land in Oregon, meditating. It must be around 1989, when I am studying Hakomi body-centered psychotherapy, which works through the medium of being present in your body and mindful of what emotions and thoughts come up.*

*As a devotee of Green Tara at the time, the Great Mother of wisdom and compassion in the Tibetan Buddhist tradition, I am used to visualizing Tara sitting in meditation, her right foot forward, ever ready to spring into action to liberate those in need. So imagine my surprise when another Goddess comes striding up to me in my meditation.*

*It is Kwan Yin, appearing out of the blue. I recognize her immediately, probably from the classic portrait of her sitting with one knee drawn up and the other leg outstretched, her foot resting on the ground, so fully relaxed and in her body. She walks right up to me, turns, and without a word, leads me deeper into the forest. I simply follow her. We come to a clearing where she sits me down in front of a large rounded rock, with my back to it.*

# She Appears!

*Then, standing beside me, she supports my body in her arms, and leans me backward onto the rock. My head is now hanging upside-down, face up. My back is pressed along the slope of the rock, with my chest arching up and over the curve at the top. Standing behind me now, she lifts my arms up over my head, and cradles my upturned hands in hers. Taking hold of both my wrists, she gives a swift gentle tug, and my heart cracks open!*

*I literally hear the snap and feel the instantaneous release in the center of my breastbone. A surge of energy breaks free from my heart like floodwaters from a dam, as years/lifetimes of pent-up sorrow, grief, and anger gush out. A rush of tears, deep despair, and unknown anguish roar through me. After who knows how long, the tumult is spent and finally settles down into a vibrantly pulsing sense of peace and joy. I am totally in my body now, resting on the earth, my heart wide open to the sky. Whew!*

*When I open my eyes, Kwan Yin is gone. I find myself back in the spot where I sat down to meditate. I lie back on a mossy bed of soft earth and welcome the feel of warm sun sinking into my skin. I see the dance of light and shadows filtering through the fir forest all around me, and fall into a deep sleep, with the sound of a gentle breeze whispering love.*

# Kwan Yin of Cascadia – Textile Art by Marcia Schenkel

Artist Marcia Schenkel, like Musawa, lives in a region of lush green woodlands, though far from Oregon, in Madison, Wisconsin. She created her "Kwan Yin of Cascadia" in 2001 as a Master's degree project at Naropa/University of Creation Spirituality in Oakland, California. In her depiction, she evokes Kwan Yin tall as a mountain, lifting her arm with its gauzy, fog-like sleeve to raise the sun above the peaks. The majestic figure radiates gentle protectiveness.

The piece is a *thangka*, a painting sewn onto cloth and meant to hang on the wall. For her Master's presentation, Marcia displayed it in a 10-foot by 10-foot tent along with devotional hangings, prayer flags, and a floor cloth honoring Gaia. Referencing both the earth and the spirit of female wisdom, Marcia called her installation "Sanctum GeoSophia."

**Kwan Yin of Cascadia**, Marcia Schenkel

# Of Dragonfly Dreams and Twilight Meditations – Paintings by Willow B. Norris

Returning to the watery realm of Mary Kelly's "Kwan Yin of Putuo Shan," artist Willow B. Norris shows Kwan Yin watching over splendidly spotted carp. Norris, who lives and works in Hawaii, often depicts Kwan Yin or the Buddha in her paintings. Her artwork evokes the verdant richness of these Pacific islands. This painting, "Dragonfly Dream VII: Listening to Peace at the Fish Pond," conveys tranquility, immersion in the world of insects, blossoms, water, and fish, juxtaposed with the mystery of stars in a night sky.

On viewing this image, author and spiritual teacher Joanna Macy said, "Amid the chaos of life, these fish swiftly passing, dragonflies hovering, Kwan Yin sits so peacefully. Seeing this is like looking into one's true nature."

**Dragonfly Dream VII:
Listening to Peace at the
Fish Pond,**
Willow B. Norris

In Norris's "Twilight Meditation," we see the same Kwan Yin, faced away from us now, perched as if at the edge of a chasm from which a golden light rises to meet the crescent moon. Blossoms ring the page. The figure suggests a peaceful reverie.

Twilight Meditation, Willow B. Norris

# On My Walk Today – Memoir by Gayle Wilde

Those who have taken on the vocations of social work, nursing, police work, and counseling, sometimes find themselves overwhelmed by the immensity of human cruelty and carelessness. In the following segment, Gayle Wilde, a mother, grandmother, and shamanistic practitioner in Olympia, Washington, recalls an experience when, working as a professional in behavioral health, she had reached her limit, a point at which she herself was injured by her work. In her story, she tells how she has learned to heal herself by inviting the presence of Kwan Yin in a sacred grove of trees, and how she brings her helplessness to an image of the goddess, to ask for strength.

Gayle writes:

*After a number of years working with child abuse survivors and child abusers, domestic violence survivors and perpetrators, drug addicts and people with mental health issues and PTSD, I fell apart. I was diagnosed with Secondary Trauma Stress Disorder. I had to quit my job to recover. Part of my recovery was finding ways to deal with the overwhelming reality of human suffering. I had many feelings of hopelessness, despair, and anger. Here in Olympia, Washington, I started walking in my neighborhood and found a beautiful natural area, and a Buddhist temple with a statue of Kwan Yin. It became my practice to walk through the natural area and arrive at the statue of Kwan Yin, where I turned the sufferings of the world over to her to heal, and to acknowledge that this was the work of the Goddess of Compassion, not a human woman such as me.*

### One
*Today, feeling crushed by the far-reaching extent and burden of human suffering, I go out for my daily walk to see Kwan Yin. Normally, I take a detour through an undeveloped area near my house. I have come into the habit of standing on a little bridge as I enter this place, taking the time to touch*

*my own feelings, to report this to the living breathing beings who live there, and to ask them if it's okay if I enter. I do this today. As I stand there, I am honest. I say, "I am feeling great fear and great anger today. I would like to come in for what healing you have to offer me, and to offer what healing I hold in return." I stand and wait, and eventually I hear some birds singing and sense it's okay for me to come in. In this natural area, I have discovered a sacred grove of cedar trees. There are six cedar trees in a circle; one of them is off by herself a bit, a sentinel overlooking a marshy patch. There are also three Douglas firs there, and one large, old alder tree. To come into this circle, I have to bow down under bent branches of vine maple.*

*The grove feels very alive today, and powerful. I walk around and touch the trees. I especially like to greet the sentinel, who holds some bells in one of her branches; they were my brother's and I tied them in the branch so they would ring free when the wind blows.*

*I decide that today I will sit on the ground and meditate. I sit in the circle, with four of the cedars around me. It's hard to describe how intimate I feel with them. I scrape some leaves out of one of the roots, smiling as I tell the tree that I am cleaning between his toes.*

*I only sit for a moment before I hear the trees telling me to lie down. I did this a lot as a child. The earth is like a poultice for me, a magnet pulling all the pain and sorrow out. The earth is vast, her healing energies reassuringly large. I lie down. Immediately, I find that I start praying for someone—someone I hardly know who helped me out in an unexpected and serendipitous way, an acquaintance who was a mirror for me, who showed me my own closed and sorrowful heart. As I lie there, I feel my heart as a portal of love, and I hold this portal open as I pray for this person. The more I lie there on the earth, praying for this person's healing, the more my heart feels beautifully open and tender.*

*I pray for myself, my own healing, my own opening. I feel the pain and sorrow letting go into Mother Earth and I am so grateful again for her vastness, for her beautiful and healing heart.*

*I breathe, I pray, I sigh, I let go. Eventually I get up, say goodbye to the trees and head down the path. I run into a couple of young alders entwined with one another. I noticed them the other day; they are so sweet. Today I just come up and hug them, my heart embracing them and their coupled sweetness.*

*As I walk down the path, I see a vision of the person I was praying for, falling into the portal of my heart, and then falling through me, beyond me, and into the heart of the divine.*

### Two

*I complete my walk through the trees and take the path to the Buddhist Temple. I step up to the tall white statue of Kwan Yin. Beneath her feet, goldfish swim. There are flowers and oranges before her, and incense is burning on the altar at her feet. I stand before her and say her name. I tell her, as always, that I need her to take this burden of human suffering from me, that truly it belongs to her, that it is her job, not mine, and it's a job I can't handle. As I stand there, I see how true this is. I am not the Goddess of Compassion, just a human woman. I ask her to look out for, and feel compassion for, all the people I know who have suffered. I name a few whose names come to me. I feel the sensation of giving over responsibility for these people and their suffering to her; I feel how the sense of responsibility rolls off my shoulders. I breathe easier, and it comes to me how completely capable she is of handling all this, and how completely I am not.*

*I bow down to her, saying out loud that I bow down to human suffering, and I bow down to compassion. I honor all that is, by bowing down to it. Suffering overwhelms me; although I don't like it or understand it, although I don't want it to exist, I bow down to it. I acknowledge its existence, and this in itself frees up some room for me to stop feeling as though it is falling on me and crushing me.*

*Turning to walk away from Kwan Yin, from the temple, I go back among the trees, grateful that each visit to her has helped me heal.*

# Aspiration – Painting by Lorraine Capparell

Lorraine Capparell is a painter, sculptor and photographer who has traveled widely in Asia, studying Buddhist and Hindu sculpture, painting, and temple architecture. Now a resident of Palo Alto, California, she finds inspiration for her art in Mother Nature, in her dreams, in her communication with close friends, and in the imagery of Eastern religions, especially Buddhism. "I make art to pay tribute to the spirit within," she says.

In this watercolor, echoing Marcia Schenkel's "Green Kwan Yin of Cascadia" in its rugged landscape, Lorraine depicts Kwan Yin as a mountain. The bodhisattva is seated in the knee-up posture of the Kansas City statue. Her towering bulk radiates the solidity of the earth, a massive comforting presence. No doubt she knows that the tiny mountain climbers are making their way up her leg and hand, and she makes no move to help or hinder. The painting is titled "Aspiration," inviting us to cultivate in ourselves the grounded, peaceful presence of Kwan Yin.

# She Appears!

**Aspiration**, Lorraine Capparell

# Kwan Yin and the Tree of Life – Memoir, Photograph, and Painting by Elaine Chan-Scherer

Elaine Chan-Scherer, a fourth-generation Chinese-American woman, lives in San Francisco, where she works as a psychotherapist and raises her family. She records her artistic exploration of the ancient symbol of the Tree of Life. This effort came at a time when one of her beloved daughters was about to leave home, leading Elaine to a Kwan Yin who exists in close relationship with nature and humans, and can ease even the most wrenching separation.

The Tree of Life, a motif depicting the connection of all forms of creation, appears in many cultures and countries from the Middle East to China, from Europe and Africa to the indigenous cultures of the Americas. A range of religious and mythological contexts evoke the Tree of Life, often suggesting fertility, immortality, and evolutionary descent. The Tree restores harmony to creation, connecting earth and sky; the Kabbalah, or Jewish mystical writings, depict it in the form of interconnected nodes.

When Chan-Scherer took on the challenge of painting a Tree of Life, she drew upon Kwan Yin and Kabbalah imagery; and her creative efforts led her to greater acceptance, as well as a deeper appreciation of Kwan Yin in association with the earth itself.

Elaine writes:

*I was taking a year-long painting class in which we studied, connected with, wrote about, and painted a different aspect of the Madonna or Divine Feminine every month. Last month, August, the subject was the Tree of Life. Being a procrastinator at heart, I usually get into a bit of a panic at the end of the month and then the painting comes through. Well, here I was in mid-August, and still no Madonna/Tree of Life painting.*

Concurrently, my oldest daughter, who had just graduated from college, was getting ready to leave home for an eleven-month internship in Taiwan. No coming home for Thanksgiving or Christmas. I realized this was probably a big deal for me as her mother (having to say goodbye for a year), but the way I was dealing with it was through distraction and busy-ness. I successfully buried my grief and anxiety and had no idea what I should be "doing" as a mother in this situation.

The weekend before Sabine was going to leave, we decided to go for a walk. We went off our usual path and found a huge tree with roots sticking out all around. Sabine sat on one of the roots and I took some pictures. When I got home, I realized this was the model for my Tree of Life painting. Yay!

**Photo of Sabine at the Tree**, Elaine Chan-Scherer

*I painted a madonna-ish version of Sabine sitting by the tree; but I am not that great a painter, so she ended up looking like a flamenco dancer. When I showed the painting to my classmates, a couple thought she looked like Kwan Yin. I wondered what Kwan Yin had to do with the Tree of Life. I sat and pondered.*

*While I was painting, I noticed an old Kwan Yin statue that I have had for a while. I bought this statue from a close-out sale at the mom-and-pop store down the street. She was a traditional Chinese Kwan Yin, very simple, made of porcelain, like something my grandmother would have had. I looked at the statue and saw that I could change my flamenco dancer into Kwan Yin using this image as a guide.*

*After the painting was done, I felt a sense of peace. Sabine sitting at the tree had been transformed into Kwan Yin. Kwan Yin was one with Sabine. She was sitting on the roots, going deep into Mother Earth, telling me my daughter and I would be connected to Mother Earth, even if we were half a world apart. Tears streamed as I realized I was releasing my daughter to a power greater than me, and that Kwan Yin would be (and already was, in fact) holding Sabine and holding me.*

*On the day of Sabine's leave-taking, I was able to be present with her. Trusting, connected to Mother Earth and my daughter, I felt my sadness but also my pride and wonder that my baby was now ready to fly.*

*After my daughter left, the painting took on a life of its own. I used the image to get grounded, to sit next to the image of Kwan Yin and follow the tree's roots deep into the earth. I noticed the nook between Kwan Yin and the tree, and I used this image in healing meditations with friends and for myself. Sitting in that nook next to Kwan Yin brought me calm and ease, even in the midst of desperation, despondency, and depression. Kwan Yin, never a remote figure, had become even more accessible to me and to my friends.*

**Painting of Tree with Kwan Yin/Sabine,** Elaine Chan-Scherer

# The Passion and Compassion of Pele/Kwan Yin – Painting by Francene Hart

Artist Francene Hart, like Willow Norris, makes her home in Hawaii. She moved there after living for many years in the woodlands of northern Wisconsin with her husband and son. In the Midwest, she responded strongly to nature, and she brings that resonance to her life in Hawaii, where she creates art that celebrates nature's wisdom. "Listening to the voices of nature helped me find my own artistic voice," she says. "The trees and animals, the water and rocks, sun and wind, moon and stars all speak clearly if we take time to listen."

Francene lives on the side of a volcano, so it makes sense she would want to portray the great Hawaiian goddess Pele, whose long hair is often depicted as black lava flowing down the sides of a mountain. But she is also strongly drawn to the ocean. "When I came to Hawaii, I considered myself a non-swimmer, yet have since become a 'born again mermaid.' Being in the ocean and swimming with her multitude of creatures, including the spinner dolphins and sea turtles, has become an important part of my personal wellness and one of the greatest joys I have experienced. I have also come to realize that this salty medium is the planetary superconductor and that as we 'pray peace' and offer the vibration of universal love into the ocean, it is quickly transmitted around the world. Imagine the possibilities."

A world traveler and spiritual seeker in many disciplines, Hart is aware that we exist in a multi-dimensional reality, and uses her art to bridge distances and show unlikely correspondences. She intends for her art to serve as a catalyst for healing and transformation.

In this "Pele/Kwan Yin" painting, she merges the passion of the tumultuous Pele with the compassion of Kwan Yin. She depicts the mountain goddess above, the water goddess below, uniting them around a mandala of golden hearts to form, she says, a "generator, which, when guided by love, will transform the world."

# She Appears!

**Passion and Compassion:**
**Pele/Kwan Yin,**
Francene Hart

# Kwan Yin of the Desert – Painting by unknown artist

A Mystery Woman created the following painting. It resides in the Mojave Desert, at the Dhamma Dena Desert Vipassana Center, a Buddhist meditation retreat founded and led by Ruth Denison, pioneer Buddhist teacher. Ruth was my first teacher, and Dhamma Dena is my spiritual home, so I have spent many a lunch hour gazing at this painting on the dining room wall. I have not been able to discover the painter's true name (the signature can be read as initials JK or VK or M, followed by last name Hausmenstamm, or Heussenstamm, or Heussmenstamm), but Ruth Denison remembers the story of its creation very well.

Ruth tells of a new meditator, a painter, who was attending a silent retreat at Dhamma Dena. She was distracted and anxious, not able to concentrate or sit still to meditate. In response to her suffering, and always ready to innovate, Ruth suggested she take some painting supplies that happened to be there at the center and go into the desert alone to paint what she saw.

This image, photographed by Carol Newhouse, a longtime student of Ruth's, is one of a series this anonymous painter produced over the course of the retreat. It captures the serenity of the desert landscape, showing Kwan Yin, herself a mountain on the horizon, tenderly watching over the Joshua trees scattered across the sandy soil. Her hand gesture signals "Fear not."

**Kwan Yin of the Desert,**
Anonymous

# Chapter Three
# When Illness Strikes

When I learned that I had cancer, I found it extremely helpful to have spent that concentrated time on Kwan Yin's island a few months earlier. The presence of the bodhisattva on that early morning beach, in waves and sunshine, breeze and beetles, and in my own body, stayed with me and strengthened me in the long bleak months of surgery and weekly chemotherapy. I felt how faithfully she teaches us to love and nurture ourselves in illness as well as health. So strongly associated with nature, Kwan Yin invites us to open to the natural rhythms of growth and decay, and can help to establish us in gentle acceptance of physical suffering, whether our own or others'.

Supported by my connection to Kwan Yin, I found myself turning toward the pain and disability rather than trying to pull away. Each morning before I began my day, while I cooked the oatmeal that was almost the only food I could eat, I listened to an audiotape called "She Carries Me." Composed by Jennefer Berezan, it is a chant calling upon Kwan Yin, "she who hears the cries of the world," lasting 23 minutes. The resonant voices, the words repeated over and over, calmed me. I felt steadied and accompanied by someone wiser and more compassionate than myself. When the chant was done and I sat carefully swallowing small bites of cereal, I felt ready to do whatever was required of me that day: to be driven to the hospital to receive the injection of chemotherapy, to teach a class, to choke down some dinner, to fall gratefully into bed. She was with me, helping me absorb the physical pain of the chemo needle, the exhaustion, and the ever-incipient nausea.

Our bodies react to bacteria and chemicals; our bones break; an alien growth can take over and consume a larger being. In the same way a horde of hungry insects can eat away the living heart of an oak tree, cancer can debilitate and destroy the life of a human being. This coming-into-being and going-out-of-being is the way of all that lives. Kwan Yin teaches me that I am an expression of this vast energy of evolving life. She shows me that I can be present to the changes in a situation and find my way, incrementally, by accepting, even if only imperfectly and momentarily, what is going on in this instant.

In Buddhism, there are said to be six worlds. These are the mental realms we inhabit, sometimes cycling among them all in a single day, alternating the god realm with the jealous god realm, the animal realm with the hell realm, and the hungry ghost realm with the human realm. In some paintings of these states of consciousness, in each segment we see a small figure standing, as if patiently waiting. This is Kwan Yin, present in each of our mental/physical conditions, offering herself, willing to be of use. If you wish to call upon her, she will accompany you through the obstacles and challenges of illness.

The following stories and images make this accompaniment real. For each of the artists and writers Kwan Yin appeared differently, for to each she offered a unique quality of comfort, healing energy, coping, and hope.

But I want to begin with my own experience, from being diagnosed with third-stage colon cancer and undergoing major surgery, to the 26 weeks of chemotherapy I endured. On one particular night of this horrendous year, I found myself in the emergency room of a crowded Oakland hospital. I arrived there after a long week of not eating and regular retching, my body reacting against the chemo. But it was there that Kwan Yin's subtle, light, and whimsical presence carried me through an almost unbearable experience.

# Thirteen Hours – Memoir by Sandy Boucher

Like a mist rising in a curtain from the surface of a deep, black pond, I rise up into voices, slabs of hard sound, scrapes of metal, thuds, and clinks. I realize I am lying on my side. Just across from me, looking back at me from another wheeled table in this huge brightness that allows us no modest hiding of blemish or sag, is a man whose mahogany-colored skin gathers the light at his naked leg. We are like two reclining figures on a tomb. He is trying to pull himself to a sitting position, elbows jabbing air, hospital gown falling back from his wrinkled thigh. No one comes to help us. We're alone with each other in the bowels of Highland Hospital, in the long crowded corridor and warren of rooms called Emergency. This is the classic county hospital, last resort for those without insurance or money, crowded, understaffed, and noisy.

An intern clutching a clipboard joins us. She has a lovely Asian face—like Kwan Yin, I think. I am touched, feeling how appropriate it is that she has materialized here.

"What symptoms are you having?" she asks me.

I can't quite manage a response. For five days I was injected with a daily dose of chemotherapy, after which I began to vomit and couldn't stop: Didn't I already tell two groups of interns about this?

I lie back, imagining this white-coated young woman in the elaborate headdress and flowing robe of the bodhisattva, her dress lifted to the side by the sea wind. I see her floating above the surf on Putuo Shan, the sacred island, as I slip slowly away from consciousness.

From that still, dark pond, I wake up again to see that the gurney across from me is now occupied by an old woman. Kindness and care have carved shallow gullies on her face. She looks as if her back and limbs are electric with pain, as she holds to the hard workman's hands of a young man who resembles her, his dark head tilted close to hers. I feel tears pooling.

"What seems to be the problem?" asks an African-American intern in a stiff snowy coat.

Yes, what is it? I ask myself. What terrible disease wracks this woman's body? How has she come to this place in such agony? Is there a shot or a pill or . . . ? I am momentarily lost in her distress.

The intern leans closer to me and raises his eyebrows. Slowly I realize he is asking about me, he is asking about my "problem."

Each time I arrive out of my darkness into consciousness, I become more aware of the noises, the endless clangs and bumps, and the raised, tight voices outside my curtained cubicle.

Next to my gurney, now, stands Deborah, a large woman with long, brown hair that falls straight down her back. She is my Kwan Yin from North Carolina, speaking in a sweet, slow accent as if she is chewing and savoring the words. Deborah tells me, because she is a nurse and knows these things, that the drug dripping into my hand has stopped the vomiting.

"And see this bag? They're puttin' fluids in you for your dehydration. I bet they'll take you upstairs to a hospital room pretty soon, and you can rest."

I had met Deborah in one of my writing workshops. She is a gifted, subtle writer and shy student. When I told the group, several months ago, that I would have surgery in a week, she spoke up with uncharacteristic force, "I'll stay overnight with you in the hospital," and I thought, aha, a bodhisattva has arrived.

On the night after my surgery, in my hospital room, Deborah had helped me into a chair and sponged me with a cloth soaked in warm soap scented with eucalyptus she had brought from home. Avoiding the ten-inch open incision that bisected my belly, being careful of the needle through which narcotic and nourishment dripped, and watching out for the tube that entered through my nose and snaked down to drain brown acids from my stomach, she had drawn the soft wet rag over my skin. My body, utterly vulnerable after the assault of surgery, had surrendered to her touch. I had felt a deep, voluptuous pleasure, powerful in itself but enhanced by the awareness that I was alive still, that my body could still feel something other than pain. Deborah had toweled me dry, changed the linen on my hospital bed, helped me back into it, and pulled the clean-smelling sheet up over my chest.

Kwan Yin had arrived yet again, speeding from her South China island to inhabit Deborah's body and guide her gentle hands. Much lore centers on Kwan Yin's hands and arms: the thousand-armed Kwan Yin, ready to reach out and avert every disaster, grant every wish; the celebrated Princess Miao Shan who gave up her arms and eyes to save her father's life; the ancient Chinese myth of her statue, missing its right arm, that came sailing across the sea to a little village and prevailed on a carpenter there to carve her a new arm. I was bathed in gratitude for these helping hands and arms as I sank away into sleep.

Now, months later, here in the Emergency department of Highland, Deborah once again has come to help me. I look up into her round, kind, smiling face, feel her hand stroking my arm. She rolls her eyes toward some new uproar in the hall outside the curtain, and says, "I guess you been havin' some night, huh?"

I feel my lips pulling up into a rueful smile. "I guess so."

Deborah shakes her head. "Well, I just want to tell you that all hospitals aren't like this."

She knows that although I am almost sixty years old and have worked for doctors, until the cancer got me I have never been a patient in a hospital. She knows Highland was my only refuge and that I have no standard to which to compare it. I guess she thinks I will be reassured to know that not all hospitals vibrate with such urgency.

But after this long night, I feel like a creature whose true environment is this hospital's lower depths, this ground-floor emergency room. The floors of the hospital rise above me. Hundreds of people move and talk, bend and lift, touch roughly or with practiced tenderness as I lie here in the fundament. I can't imagine being anywhere else, but here, absorbed into this giant body.

Yet, I wonder about the passage of time, impossible to gauge in this fluorescent eternity.

"Deborah, how late is it?"

## She Appears!

She lifts her hand from my arm to look at her big-faced nurse's watch. "It's 3:30 in the morning."

I stare in astonishment at her as I calculate. Friends brought me to the hospital twelve hours ago! The thought plunges me into a puddle of weakness, my Jell-O body melting. And yet my head, arms, and chest buzz, perhaps from the drug they've been giving me, maybe from the tension so palpable around me, maybe from not having any nourishment for seven days, except this drip of liquid. I know I am in an unusual condition, unhinged by the anguish I have seen and heard.

I try to focus on my breath, to experience the flow of warm air over my upper lip as I inhale, to feel the touch of air on my nostrils, to experience life where it is actually taking place. Suddenly, a doctor appears. He is erect, brisk, blond with little mouse-tufts of gray at his temples. Is this a senior doctor, or yet another in the parade of interns who have looked in on me?

He consults the clipboard he lifts from my gurney.

"Well, Ms. Boo-cher, looks like you're stabilized. No more vomiting from that chemo. I'll get the nurse to send you upstairs, and we'll keep you until tomorrow to make sure you're done with all that."

Zing of curtain whipping open, and a nurse enters. She looks dead-tired but determined.

"They'll be sending someone down for you soon. Till then, I'm putting you in the hallway."

The hallway! Deborah looks as stricken as I feel.

"Oh no, please," I beg. "Not the hallway. Don't put me there."

"It won't be long," the nurse answers. She leans to release the brake on the gurney, and I find myself gliding out of my curtained haven, a sacrificial victim in a shaman's canoe, pushed from shore into the crocodile-infested stream.

Gurneys line the walls of this bright, loud corridor. Nurses and interns rush through a collision course of crutches and wheelchairs and IV stands. Patients lie, swollen, bloodied, with great angry bruises, wearing patches of gauze hastily stuck over the holes in their skins. They are rent, opened, struck down by a cramping heart, a drug-induced mental full-stop. Some twist and moan. Policemen lounge at the entrance, radiating boredom and authority.

The nurse parks my gurney against the wall, and I am becalmed in this new place whose noises I have been hearing for so many hours. The wings in my chest flutter to a halt, leaving an expectant silence in their wake. Deborah, my faithful bodhisattva, my Appalachian Kwan Yin, finds a chair and sits with her arm next to my pillow. Together we gaze over this wreckage of broken, beaten people.

The gurney just in front of me is occupied by a raw-boned blond woman. She is, perhaps, in her forties, a jeans-clad, hard-luck looking woman with puffy purpled face and stiff bleached hair. She's sitting up, but her wrists and ankles are held tight to the metal bars by thick leather straps.

"God damn you, let me up! I've pee'd my pants! I'm sittin' here in my own piss." Her voice, thick and metallic, grates.

"Nurse!" she shouts to someone pushing past her, "You got to let me up! Unfasten me!" And she jerks her arms against the straps.

"On her way to the psych ward," mutters the nurse as he passes. "Tried to kill somebody and then herself."

I feel a quaking inside. I can't stand this. I can't stand any more suffering. All night I've been filled and filled with it, and now I have room for no more.

"Help!" she shouts. "Let me up off here!"

Her frenzy enters me and pushes against the last fragile threads of my control. It hurts more than I can believe. And then something trembles, rips, and falls away, and I feel myself pass through. I am in a realm where all is wide and still. I have lost what solidity I had and become a shower of musical notes tinkling like glass in the silence. I sense the vast spaciousness of the bodhisattva. This must be the realm that Kwan Yin inhabits, beyond my limited perceptions and expectations, beyond boundaries.

This is more intense than the penetration I have sometimes entered in meditation, where I have been aware of my body as atoms gyrating, as waves of energy endlessly passing through. No, this is something else. This is as if all of me has been lifted out into a vast space that is both inside of me and outside, containing me. The space encompasses every person and object, sound and smell, holding all in exquisite, pleasurable suspension. Something frail and intricately witty pulses through my cells.

I look into Deborah's brown eyes, questioning; she smiles, and I believe she is here with me in this same condition.

I sink back, aware of nothing I could want that could match this fullness. A plethora of joys vibrates in the huge space I inhabit and have become. I look around me, seeing the tired, tense faces of the nurses and the young interns, the man lying deathly still with a huge white bandage on his head, the young man in the wheelchair huddling over his bloody leg, the woman clutching a sobbing child. Their suffering enters this spaciousness and hovers, held in a radiance of infinite tenderness, cradled in Kwan Yin's vast compassionate embrace.

The woman on the gurney before me continues to rant. "You fuckers, you get me off this thing and let me go to the bathroom! I'm sittin' in a god-damned puddle, damn you, I'm gonna flood this whole damned hallway!"

She does not know that Deborah and I are laughing. Helpless before this torrent of words, we have slipped beyond suffering and compassion and bodies and instruments. Giggling, we acknowledge the limitless absurdity of all of it, including ourselves: I with the big scar in my belly and veins full of chemicals, Deborah who has come to help and plunged with me into this cauldron, among the interns who are punchy with fatigue, the harried nurses and clerks, the restless policemen who want no more than to write their reports and leave. We are all shimmering in this heightened light, lifted up by the Goddess of Compassion, gone far beyond our minds and bodies into the immense loving embrace of the universe.

# One–Breasted Kwan Yin – Painting by Kimberly Eve Snyder

Cancer, if we survive it, can leave us scarred or compromised. Many women live with one breast or with both breasts removed; some disguise their flat chest and scar with a prosthesis, some proudly reveal it or even draw attention to it with a tattoo, some have the missing breast reconstructed. Artist Kimberly Eve Snyder, or Jaia, has painted a Kwan Yin with one breast in honor of breast cancer survivors.

Jaia, who lives part-time in Florida, part-time in Massachusetts, gave the original of this painting to a woman who runs a store in Provincetown, Massachusetts. Called Recovering Hearts, the shop provides a space for regular Alcoholics Anonymous meetings and also supports women recovering from breast cancer and mastectomies

The naked breast in images of deities traditionally suggests eternal beauty and nourishment. Inspired by a cave painting in China, Kimberly's one-breasted Kwan Yin expresses acceptance of the beauty and aliveness of the female body as it may be after surgery.

**One-Breasted Kwan Yin**, Kimberly Eve Snyder

## Passing It On – Memoir by Yvonne MacKenzie

A number of women have remarked that, after experiencing Kwan Yin's compassion, they were able to act in a more caring fashion toward others. Even writing about Kwan Yin can bring this result. In the daylong Kwan Yin retreats I lead, we explore compassion, and we write, and then share, the ways we have experienced that quality in our lives. Perhaps we received or gave compassion gladly; perhaps we tensed up and could not reach out with our kindness; perhaps we rejected help, or were afraid to admit to our vulnerability. In this exploration, we touch into that place where people meet without pretense or defenses, desiring only to serve life. Participants sometimes report that, after writing and sharing, they feel more comfortable thinking of themselves as compassionate people and more likely to act in a caring way toward others.

Yvonne MacKenzie, who was born in Scotland and immigrated to Canada, is a poet who has worked in social-service jobs. She lives on an island with her cat and her son. Yvonne describes her response to Kwan Yin and the stunning hospital visitation that opened her to a more whole-hearted compassion in both her personal and professional lives.

Yvonne writes:

*Kwan Yin has figured prominently in my life since the first time a friend, returning from a meditation retreat, showed me a picture of her face. Mysteriously, I burst into tears as soon as I set eyes on her serene expression. Without knowing anything about her, I felt a deep connection and knew immediately she would be a spiritual guide.*

*After my friend explained her significance as a bodhisattva of compassion, I realized how badly I yearned for her example of empathy and service. As a child, I'd always been moved by the suffering of others and wanted to somehow alleviate the pain and rectify the ills of the world. When I was a young adult working in the justice system as a para-legal/social worker, I was a passionate advocate for social change, yet profoundly discouraged by the ignorance and indifference of those in power. As well, I felt tainted by my own anger and frustration; I perceived it as an inner violence that was both equivalent to the abuses I opposed and at odds with my spiritual principles.*

*One day, I found myself writhing in excruciating abdominal pain and ended up in hospital having emergency surgery for a ruptured fallopian cyst. Compounding the physical discomfort was the disheartening prognosis that I would likely be unable to have children.*

*The day after the operation, I was lying in my hospital bed all bandaged up and hooked up to an intravenous line, overwhelmed with fear and despair. I drifted off into an altered state, not really asleep, yet not fully awake. I remember feeling enveloped by a sensation of extraordinary peace and calm. In my mind's eye, I saw Kwan Yin at the foot of my bed, smiling radiantly. Her hands were placed in the gestures expressing "have no fear," and "let the earth witness this truth."*

*She guided me in a gentle healing exercise similar to the opening moves of Tai Chi, which I knew nothing about at the time. I had been told I would be bedridden and medicated for at least a week before being even minimally mobile again. I had been told I would need a few weeks of recovery time before I would be able to leave the hospital.*

*Imagine the surprise of the ward nurse when she found me standing beside my bed, peacefully and comfortably breathing from the belly and doing some kind of Oriental exercise. This was back in the early eighties when the Western medical world was pretty skeptical about alternative modalities.*

*Despite the admonishment of the nursing team and specialists, I continued to follow my own healing program and to meditate on the image of Kwan Yin. Four days later, I was released. I still had staples in my belly, was in a weakened state, and definitely needed the TLC of my partner and friends, but I felt as if I were in a state of grace.*

*That experience was a turning point in my life. I'd always believed I was on a mission of some sort, but the vision of Kwan Yin compelled me to devote myself more fully to a path of compassionate service both personally and professionally, by becoming an early childhood educator and community health worker.*

*Many years later, against heartbreaking odds, I gave birth to a precious son, a blessed gift from the goddess I revere. He entered the world as a sunny, sensitive soul. On his thirteenth birthday, rather than going surfing or skateboarding, he went to a retreat at a nearby monastery to "take refuge" in a ceremony devoted to Avalokiteshvara/Kwan Yin and Tara, the Tibetan aspects of the goddess.*

*My growth and understanding have happened in fits and starts, in a cyclical manner. Like most human beings, I've blundered a few times and repeated some mistakes until I learned the life lessons they taught me. But Kwan Yin has been the constant source of inspiration and solace on my journey.*

## Healing Kwan Yin – Painting by Max Dashu

Max Dashu, an Oakland native, is intimate with goddesses, having spent her life researching them. As an artist, writer, and videographer, she publishes books and posters, and teaches women's history and heritages. She is also no stranger to illness, having suffered from a dire, parasite-transmitted disease.

Max describes the dream encounter that inspired this powerful painting and pointed to her eventual healing:

"When I was flattened by Lyme disease, after an unusual triple seizure and in despair of ever healing, I had a dream of Kwan Yin as an amulet shot through with mother-of-pearl.

"Here is the dream: I am walking through a dark tunnel when I glimpse a bright thing in the dirt before me. I pick it up, and it turns out to be an ivory Kwan Yin, crowned by a pearl. Her blessing opens new possibilities. Life force flows into the receptive hand, while the other paints the dream. This dream was an omen of grace and future healing."

**Healing Kwan Yin,**
Max Dashu

# Kwan Yin: A Presence in my Heart – Memoir and Photograph by Ursula Popp

U rsula Popp echoes Yvonne MacKenzie's gratitude to Kwan Yin for enriching her caring work with others. Ursula, who was born in Switzerland, now lives in Seattle, where she works as a healer-medicine woman and teacher. She describes her journey from her problematical relationship with the Virgin Mary in her Catholic girlhood to her awakening to Kwan Yin's energy as an adult, and she tells how she came to view the goddess as an aid and support for her therapeutic efforts.

This long process involved a gradual transformation from Ursula's petitioning Kwan Yin for help, to effortlessly embodying the goddess while working with clients. Among her more penetrating perceptions has been the realization that the bodhisattva is always serene and unhurried, her compassion for others expressed not in frantic activity but in deep receptivity.

Ursula writes:

*Growing up Catholic in Switzerland, I experienced the Virgin Mary as the female figure of our faith. She was the mother of Jesus, a kind, loving, and compassionate intermediary between the sinful me and her son, the Son of God. Though highly revered, she wasn't seen as a goddess, not divine herself, but only as a conduit for divine grace. As a girl, I was a tomboy, full of energy and curious about everything. I preferred to head for the woods than to help my mother darn my father's socks. Though I was drawn to the Virgin's softness, calm, and patience, accepting her as a role model seemed impossible and unattractive. I didn't understand how she could be a virgin, and why that would make her particularly revered.*

*"Don't you love Mary?" I was asked as a child in my very religious family and at church services. "She can teach you how to grow into a dutiful woman. It is more important to help others than follow your own desire for adventure and fun."*

# She Appears!

*But to me, the Virgin's life felt like a life half lived, nothing I aspired to. I wanted more than motherhood, and turned away from the Virgin Mary. I wasn't willing to pull in the reins, not before I let them go for the adventure I hoped life held for me.*

*I first encountered Kanzeon, as Kwan Yin is called in Japanese, when I was 35 years old and had begun to meditate in the Zen tradition. In 1986, during the first of many week-long silent retreats, I learned the Japanese chant to Kanzeon. One of the assistant teachers would hit a wooden shell with a stick, keeping the heart rhythm of the sutra, as we repeated the words every day seven times. Sitting cross-legged on my cushion, I enjoyed my voice after a day of silence, reciting the chant with fervency, not caring about the meaning of the Japanese words:*

*Kanzeon*
*Namu Butsu*
*Yo Butsu u in*
*Yo Butsu u en*

*I fell in love with a painting of Kwan Yin that hung outside the Zen hall. It depicts her in what's known as the "royal ease pose," with one leg crossed in front of her, the other knee bent, one arm resting on that knee almost lazily. The idea that the goddess of compassion could sit at ease while truly hearing those suffering and not run around all day long trying to solve their problems was calming to me, and relieved me of pressure to do good. [Editor's note: See the 12th century statue in Chapter One.]*

*I'd made peace with the Virgin Mary and had let go of the patriarchal role that the Catholic Church had constructed for her. Kwan Yin seemed less convoluted to me, and I began turning to her for help when I felt distressed.*

*I created an altar in my back yard, a waterfall over which she presides, symbolically pouring healing water onto the earth. I hoped she'd help calm and center my clients even before they entered my office. As a holistic health practitioner, I use an integrated approach of counseling, cranio-sacral therapy, and East Asian Medicine to assist my patients in gaining physical and emotional strength and well-being.*

*Kwan Yin was, at first, someone external to me, an image to turn to when I needed help, not a figure I could aspire to emulate. But a few years after I designed my back yard, I began to notice*

*Kwan Yin's effect on my internal life. I attended a retreat for healers in California, a diverse group of women, most of them new to me, all gathered around a teacher, all recognizing the need to tend to and heal ourselves from time to time so we could continue our healing work with others.*

*One day, a woman at the retreat talked about her parents, who'd been fortunate enough to escape Nazi Germany in the thirties. She wept as she described how conflicted she was about everything German. Although she was of German descent, the German people had done horrific things and hurt her family beyond imagination.*

*"My mother used to speak to me in German," she said tearfully. "But I hate everything German, and so did she. My grandparents were killed in the camps! My mother got away, at least her body did and we should all be grateful. But her soul, her happiness, and her trust in life had been killed. Still now, over seventy years later, she's riddled with guilt for having escaped. I can't bear to see her this way. I'm so angry all the time and helpless, I just want to jump out of my skin."*

*Barely able to breathe, she sobbed inconsolably, her voice wavering between deep sorrow and spiteful anger. I found myself moving across the room to her. Folding this bundle of pain and sorrow into my arms, I rocked her back and forth. To comfort her, I began singing a lullaby in German. It was a song I hadn't thought of in decades.*

*Schlaf Kindlein, schlaf! / Sleep, little child sleep!*
*Der Vater hütet d'Schaf / Father guards the sheep,*
*Die Mutter schüttelt's Bäumelein / Mother shakes the little tree,*

# She Appears!

*Da fällt herab ein Träumelein / A little dream drops out for thee*
*Schlaf, Kindlein, schlaf! / Sleep, little child, sleep!*

*Gradually, her tense body relaxed. Finally, she reached over my arms to hold onto me, growing calm at last. The room and the women around us disappeared as we held each other in this archetypal embrace.*

*"This lullaby is so beautiful," she said after a long time, slowly drying her swollen eyes. "It is good to hear this language spoken so softly. I never imagined it was possible. It soothes my soul to the core."*

*"Kwan Yin was so present in the room when you were holding her," one of the other women told me later.*

*This comment shifted something in me. Up until then, I'd turned to Kwan Yin as a source of help and compassion for me. As a healthcare provider, I mostly do my work unobserved by others, except my patients. This woman's comment made me realize that Kwan Yin had been acting through me in my work rather than being a force outside of me. This was news to me, and very humbling. I understood that I wasn't alone in my efforts. I was supported; it wasn't all up to me. From then on, I'd glance over at the Kwan Yin icon on the altar in my treatment room for a sense of mutual effort when working with clients.*

*Over the years, I developed a broad and inclusive sense of Kwan Yin. I believe that her heart and ears are open to laughter as well as tears, joy and happiness as well as sorrow and hardship. And for me, the Virgin Mary and Kwan Yin are quite similar. Both are symbols of open-hearted, genuine care and love for all beings. And both have a place on my eclectic altar now.*

*Not long ago, I was sitting in deep meditation when a question arose within me: What is it that your heart is most deeply longing for?*

*The answer came clear and without hesitation: For all beings to awaken. An image appeared of a world without war, of communities caring for each other, and of all beings, human and non-human, living in mutual respect and deep appreciation of the natural world. A painting I had seen as a child, of the Biblical lamb and lion dwelling together, came to me with startling clarity.*

*This is Kwan Yin's longing, I realized, and felt an undeniable kinship with her. A warm sense, an unknown relaxation spread throughout my body and all ideas of separateness disappeared. In this longing, I, too, sit at ease.*

# Annunciation – Painting by Eleanor Ruckman

Artist Eleanor Ruckman, echoing Ursula Popp's revelations, brings together the Virgin Mary with an elder Kwan Yin seated in meditation, her foot dipping into flowing waters. She calls the painting "Annunciation," playing with the traditional Christian image of the angel Gabriel's coming to the Virgin to tell her she would conceive and bear a divine child. In Ruckman's version, the holy spirit/owl ancestor blesses the two female figures, announcing that we are entering a new era of care for our waters and our earth.

The figures, so tenderly juxtaposed, illustrate the experience of some of the women in this book who feel a kinship between Kwan Yin and the Virgin; they express reverence for the eternal cycle of the natural world, including our own bodies, evoking the holiness of both life and death, calling for our own healing and the healing of our environment. Ruckman, reflecting on the sacredness of female embodiment, points out that Kwan Yin's healing waters and energies flow from her lotus-womb. It is a distinctly unconventional perception of the bodhisattva, but one that connects her to the ancient veneration of the female body.

Annunciation,
Eleanor Ruckman

## I Didn't Know Her . . . But She Knew Me – Memoir by Meredith Balgley

When Meredith Balgley was 14, she survived a plane crash in which 68 percent of her body was burned. She lost her mother and two other family members in the crash. She well knows how we can seem to have healed from traumatic injuries suffered in early life, and to have put them behind us, and yet still those injuries can rise up and ask to be healed again. Meredith's tale of a spontaneously combusting statue leading to a lifelong relationship with Kwan Yin reminds us that we should always direct Kwan Yin's healing powers toward ourselves first.

Since surviving her unusually difficult adolescence, Meredith has lived a life of travel, music, dance, and adventure. She and her husband now reside in North Carolina, in the mountains near Asheville, where they home-birthed and homeschooled their two sons.

Meredith writes:

*For years, I had been looking for a Buddha statue that spoke to me. Just after Christmas, and just after my forty-ninth birthday, I found what I was looking for in a feminist spiritual bookstore in Berkeley, California. There it was at the end of a bookshelf: a large statue of Kwan Yin. I recognized it as a Chinese female goddess, and I knew immediately I should purchase it. I arranged shipment to my home in North Carolina.*

*In late January, I found a large cardboard box on my front porch. I noticed immediately that the top was torn open. Though the statue was inside, its head was broken off. I took the box into the house and called UPS; I would need pickup to come and examine the damage. The box stood near the front door to remind me to put it outside on the porch in the morning.*

*The next morning, after driving my kids to school, I returned home to take a shower. My husband was also getting ready to go out for the day. I was standing at the top of the stairs with a towel wrapped around me when we both smelled a strange burning smell. There was smoke pouring out of the box with the statue! My husband took it out the front door and it immediately burst into flames!*

*We were both amazed, and had no idea what could have caused this. But later (after my husband had thrown water on the box to quench the fire), I began to think about this. I am a burn survivor. A statue of the goddess Kwan Yin had spontaneously burst into flames in my home. Whatever had caused it, this event might have something to tell me. I wasn't sure if I wanted to own this statue, as it was clearly very powerful. Yet over the next few days, after UPS had come and taken the package away, I called to try to get it back. At first they couldn't find it, and then they said they had sent it back to the store. Several weeks passed and no one could find the package. It never made it back to California. It seemed that this statue had gone through a lot to tell me something.*

*It was time for me to learn about Kwan Yin. When I had bought the statue, I had also picked up the book* Discovering Kwan Yin. *Now I sat down and read it twice in one sitting. One section said Kwan Yin comes to a person's aid when her name is recited with a sincere heart. People often appeal to her during a disaster, like a storm at sea—or a fire. "If those who hold the name of Guan Shi Yin Bodhisattva should fall into a great fire, the fire will not burn them, because of Guan Shi Yin Bodhisattva's awesome spiritual power."*

*The quote spoke to me. I was burned but not consumed, the sole survivor of an accident that took my mother and two other relatives. And yes, my experience as a burn survivor had crystallized a jewel of compassion in me. A new ability was born of my suffering, a sensitivity to the suffering of others. I do hear the cries of the world, or rather I "feel" them. I have an awareness of suffering in others and a deep well of compassion. Now, after many decades of sensing, understanding, and opening my heart to people's pain, I recognize this as a gift I received though trial by fire.*

*And here was the lesson: I need to be Kwan Yin to myself, to have compassion for myself, to hear my own cries. I experienced an opening in myself. I opened the door of compassion to my own suffering.*

*After that, I did everything I could to learn about and connect with Kwan Yin, even visiting the City of Ten Thousand Buddhas in Talmage, California, where Kwan Yin is venerated. But my own Kwan Yin statue came from a surprising direction.*

*I went to see our acupuncturist, a gifted and powerful Buddhist healer from Taiwan. Many posters and statues decorate her office. On this visit, I noticed a Kwan Yin statue on the windowsill. I had no memory of seeing it before. I remarked to my mother-in-law, who was with me, that this was the kind of Kwan Yin I had been looking for. In the treatment room, as I was getting ready, I noticed a poster with a small picture from the City of Ten Thousand Buddhas monastery. When my acupuncturist came in, I said I had just visited there. She told me her brother had been there the previous week; they both did work for the monastery and were involved with the branch temple in the Bay Area.*

*She began my treatment and, as she finished putting needles in me, I told her about my burning statue experience. She looked at me deeply and asked if I had a statue to replace it and keep in my home. I told her no. I sensed a power in the room. She left the room and when she came back, she was carrying the statue from the waiting room. She said, "I am giving you this statue. I brought it with me from Taiwan thirty years ago. I felt shivers all through my body when you told me the story."*

*She told me Kwan Yin was coming to me now and I needed to let go of the past and accept Kwan Yin as my mother. Once again, I was deeply moved. I felt this gift was very powerful, not personally but spiritually. She told me how to set up an altar and gave me posters and Chinese prayer books. Later, she did blessing calligraphies for me.*

*The years have passed. My home and life have been full of my male relationships: father, brother, husband, two sons. But it is also home to Kwan Yin in many forms. She is my feminine support, my mother, my sister, and my goddess. She is also me, as I continue to learn and practice self-compassion.*

# From Rage to Tenderness – Memoir by Margaret Mann

Margaret Mann, a disabled lesbian Buddhist writer and counselor in Hawaii, was deeply in need of compassion. In Margaret's life, the randomness of misfortune, disease, and disability seemed brutally unfair. Her otherwise supportive father fell prey to mental instability that threatened the family. After acquiring her disability, Margaret became the victim of a series of painful accidents. She tells of her own rage at her disability and how that mirrored her father's uncontrolled fury.

Then, at a meditation retreat, tortured by her emotions, she called upon the *lovingkindness* of Kwan Yin to help her. Margaret's strong spirit comes through in her account of this transformative experience.

Margaret writes:

*After an idyllic childhood in Hawaii and a relatively calm adulthood in Washington, DC, I was disabled at age 52 by a small blood vessel bursting in my spinal cord, leaving me paralyzed from the waist down. My life in the sixteen years since has been, to borrow a phrase, the best of times and the worst of times. It has been the best in that I have grown spiritually in ways I am sure I never would have otherwise: I now understand Kwan Yin's compassion at a very deep level. As my life with the wheelchair progressed, it became clear that compassion for myself was at the core of all other compassion. It is no accident that lovingkindness meditation starts with oneself. I did nothing to cause my disability; no one else caused my disability; it just happened and I had to figure out a way to deal with it.*

*How it has been the worst of times may seem readily apparent. It was hard to adjust to having half the income I had before, it was hard to deal with all the agencies that were supposed to help and didn't, and it was hard to endure the pain 24/7. But a broken hip when my scooter tipped over, a broken leg when I fell down at the swimming pool, a broken ankle when I caught my foot in the door and didn't realize it, a gall bladder removal after gall stone attack, a thyroid removal after a large goiter grew there, and recurring breast cancer resulting in a double mastectomy—these were the real worst of times. Through all of this, I was alone, with no partner, with friends who came and went, living in Washington, DC, 6,000 miles from my home in Hawaii.*

*My first awareness of Kwan Yin came to me in my family. My father was an Apache/Caucasian man who embraced Zen Buddhism after moving to Hawaii in 1949. Our house burned down when I was in the third grade and he had it rebuilt as a Japanese house with tatami matting, shoji windows and the ceremonial tokunoma room with two alcoves. The white porcelain statue of Kwan Yin graced one side, standing on the shelf used for flower arrangements, and a scroll of a carp swimming upstream hung in the other alcove. Between them was a polished plum wood pole. I spent hours in that room lying on tatami matting reading books under Kwan Yin's peaceful gaze.*

*One terrible day, my father was suffering from a chemical imbalance that sent him into an out-of-control rage. He went roaring through the house smashing things left and right. I stood frozen, watching him attack the lovely Kwan Yin statue and demolish it, incredulous that he could smash the Kwan Yin, of all things, the Bodhisattva of Compassion. My younger brother and I ran into the bathroom, locked the door and held on tight to each other.*

*Shortly after I was disabled, I attended a silent retreat. I was having a hard time with my anger in the sittings; a friend, seeing my distress, put candies on my mat during a break. This act of kindness infuriated me; I threw the candies across the meditation hall, which luckily was empty. It didn't occur to me then, though it does now, that my father might have been feeling the same when he smashed the Kwan Yin statue in our home. The act of compassion was so painful and I was so out of touch with my own compassion that rage took its place.*

*When the participants reassembled, I left the hall and went to my room. But on the way there I gathered up the candies and put them in my pocket, aware at some level that these gifts were a good thing.*

*I was afraid I would scream out loud. When I got to my room, I put the pillow over my face and screamed and screamed and screamed. Finally, the screaming subsided into sobbing. I was bereft, alone, isolated, and totally miserable. As I sat there crying, little by little my Buddhist practice came back to me. The lovingkindness practice, Kwan Yin's gift to us . . . I wish for myself happiness, freedom from suffering, and compassion for my situation. Breathing in, breathing out. I remembered my father's goodness. He had often given dharma talks at the dining room table. When I was twelve, of course, I would roll my eyes and pray he would stop talking. Later, when studying Buddhism as an adult, I would hear echoes of my father's talks in the teacher's words. He had laid a good foundation for me. He was a gentle and peaceful man, except for that brief period before the medications to control his mental illness became effective.*

*After a long while, alone in my little retreat room, I stopped crying. Kwan Yin had let me see my father and me in our entirety, not just when we were out of control; now I could let go of both my reaction to his instability and my grief over my own disability. When I roused myself enough to return to the meditation hall, everything was beautiful. My fellow retreatants looked so serene, dust motes were floating in the air, a slight fragrance of incense filled my nose, and the little Buddha statue sitting on the altar looked peaceful. Breathing in, breathing out. I knew then I would survive. I kept the candies in my pocket for the rest of the retreat and on the ride home told my friend, who had put them there, about what had happened and how Kwan Yin had come to soothe me. She just smiled and nodded.*

# Chapter Four
# Mothers and Daughters

All humans share a need for the unconditional love of the mother. The first religions were based on the mystery and miracle of birth, and the first humans naturally venerated the mother-as-goddess; so it should not surprise us that our Bodhisattva of Compassion is widely seen as Great Mother Kwan Yin.

Most images of Kwan Yin portray her as a young woman: lithe, slim, conventionally beautiful, and often rather androgynous. This representation is a far cry from our pagan mothers, who are revered in women's spirituality and Wiccan circles, with their ample thighs, bellies, and breasts, so visibly suggestive of procreation and nurturance. There are, however, some paintings and sculptures that show Kwan Yin as a mature woman, and a few depict her holding a baby. She is credited with bringing infants to childless couples. Unlike the Virgin Mary, who was an actual earthly mother, Kwan Yin does not bear children, yet many people in various cultures view her as Mother Kwan Yin, the one who watches over us, guides us, and rescues us from dangerous situations.

The image of Kwan Yin as mother grows from ancient roots in Chinese society. The founder of Taoism received the basic teachings of that philosophy from his mother, who was called Holy Mother Goddess. Other early male seekers benefitted from the wisdom of divine females, and fully acknowledged them as goddesses. The Queen Mother of the West was worshipped by humble as well as exalted citizens of China. She was sometimes envisioned as an old crone with white hair, but poets called her Amah, the intimate name for nanny or wet-nurse. She protected women who lived alone, particularly older, widowed women or childless women, who were vulnerable in a culture of strong family ties. The Queen Mother was understood to be childless, yet she was the mother of all beings.

And so, when Kwan Yin arrived in Chinese religion, she had a model and lineage in the Queen Mother of the West. In later centuries, goddess figures played vibrant roles in popular novels. These fictional heroines were typically post-menopausal. Free of childbirth and no longer driven by sexual desire, they could represent pure motherliness, radiating compassionate nurturance toward the whole world.

As the prevailing deity in some Chinese religions, often led by women, Kwan Yin was believed to be a mother goddess, creator, and savior of humankind. In one, Kwan Yin was said to travel throughout the world each day, going to every home to take care of her children. She often disguised herself as a beggar woman, knocking on each door, not to beg food but to check on the people who lived in the houses and offer compassionate care.

Other models for Mother Kwan Yin appear in stories about actual or mythological old women who led exemplary lives as spiritually enlightened, physically energetic guides for those on a spiritual path. Historically, even though the roles for Chinese women in society were extremely restricted, older Chinese matriarchs often wielded considerable power within their family systems.

Kwan Yin, therefore, had many precursors in Chinese society, which led to her being viewed as Great Mother Kwan Yin, Venerable Mother Kwan Yin.

In the West, the subject of mothers and mothering exists in a highly charged atmosphere. Some of us had loving, supportive mothers, while others experienced less-than-adequate or problematical care from our mothers or mother-substitutes. Many of us have borne and raised children, or are engaged right now in the joyful, excruciating, gratifying, frustrating, and guilt-producing process of nurturing small human beings. In moments of confusion or despair, we may have longed for the steady protection of a mother-figure, the all-healing embrace of something or someone more powerful than ourselves.

As daughters, some of us may be engaged in healing unsatisfactory relationships we've had with our mothers, while others are continuing the rich contact we cherish, especially as we realize, unthinkably but inevitably, that our mothers will not always be with us. Or perhaps our mother has already passed on, leaving us to seek and recognize her presence and lingering influence in ourselves. Whatever our relationships with our mothers, Kwan Yin's compassion can inform and soften us as we explore this unique and powerful human connection.

The women in this chapter are mothers and daughters. The mothers tell of how, in dark times, they benefitted from Kwan Yin's concern, how her arrival reassured them that the painful circumstances they were suffering would change into more livable situations. The daughters who sent me their stories and artwork felt Kwan Yin's presence awakening them to their own beauty and strength, expressing the bright interest, playfulness, and openness of the bodhisattva's youthful joy. In one account, Kwan Yin saves a family from death, leaving a lasting impact on the grateful daughter. And a painting celebrates the expansive gentleness of a young island-born daughter who embodies compassion, the quality for which Kwan Yin is most universally known and revered.

## The Shower Mother – Memoir by Lesanne Brooke

Lesanne Brooke is a white South African who spent twelve years in London before returning to her roots. Back home in Africa, she birthed her babies, and went to live on a farm with her partner and children, until a recent fire destroyed their home and sent them to live in Cape Town.

Lesanne studied shamanism from her late twenties on, focusing on an experiential, earth-based, spiritual path. In London, she explored alternative therapies and processes and did healing courses at the London College of Psychic Studies. The natural homebirths of her children awoke her to new potential. "I found that this deep connection to my woman power and body radically enhanced my abilities to sense other realities and open to wisdom teachings."

All this took place in a South African cultural/political context. Lesanne felt trapped in a world-view that she knew to be untrue, which felt limiting, harsh, and alien. Her own ancestral and cultural heritage is mixed in many ways, "and I have found so much beauty in the fusion of so-called otherness or opposites. I love Africa: being a white South African is a responsibility I take seriously."

Shamanism, she notes, "is the ancient root of our culture. It existed before religious dogma and polarized segregation, expressing a simple way of being that is honoring to all." Looking for a nurturing and authentic expression of spirituality, she began working with an indigenous African teacher and learned to identify her work as African, re-membering the ancient mother-culture.

Lesanne now mentors and coaches people of all colors, ages, and creeds. In the following piece, she tells of an extraordinary apprenticeship that continued over years and led to her confidence in practicing her own unique form of motherhood. Kwan Yin arrived one day in her shower, and came back regularly to inform and guide her in her relationship with her children and the world.

Lesanne writes:

*I remember Kwan Yin as water, flowing water that cascades in a wide, soft-silky waterfall. I see her body, too: abundant, shaped like the waterfall, dancing eyes, languid smile, cross-legged, with plump, graceful hands.*

*The first time I felt her was in my late twenties. I was living in London, opening up to my spiritual journey, exploring nature and shamanism from a roof-top artist's studio flat with expansive views and beautiful light.*

*One evening, a friend gave me a massage. This friend works consciously with moving Chi through his hands. As I returned from massage-heaven and sat down for a cup of tea, I found my small body growing energetically, until it felt large and expansive. I became totally immersed in this waterfall body and then, smiling serenely from behind my eyes, languid Kwan Yin emerged. I knew it was her. Moved and unable to talk, I sat quietly stunned by delighted bliss.*

*I knew nothing about Kwan Yin; I only had the name. So I did a little research. I found pictures of her, thin and graceful. But my Kwan Yin was voluptuous and sparkling. I felt no link between my experience and the formal descriptions or pictures, so I chose to know the experience and leave the detail.*

*About ten years later, I met her again. This time she was outside of me, perched up on the edge of my shower wall. She looked down at me with all her benevolence and grace, spilling voluptuously over the wall edges as the shower water poured down onto me. Her eyes were laughing.*

*By now I was in my mid-thirties, living in Africa, and a new mother—new to the experience of natural birth and milk-abundant breasts. I was a warrior mother, initiated by my son's birth. I felt strong and tall and very open, but I also felt cracked and alien and lost in the universe. The power of my pregnancy and birth had changed me forever. I was floating in an unknown reality, utterly re-arranged and disconnected from all that I had been until the birthing moment. My ego struggled even as I surrendered to the total experience of falling in love and losing myself. I was also seriously facing the flaws in my world.*

*South African society was very autocratic and paternalistic during this era of extreme racism and apartheid, dictating the right way to do things and how things must be. I was finding that every-thing was skewed and biased to an alienating worldview, a worldview in which "freedom" meant 78 channels on TV, beauty was plastic, and we "needed" to consume excessively to be good parents/ people ("Your child might be damaged for life if you don't!"). I didn't want to be ruled by guilt and*

# She Appears!

*I didn't want my children to grow up with society's lies. I needed to experience for myself, challenge everything, and find my own truth. I was breaking many social rules and finding myself stronger for it. I was learning to listen to my body, my children, and nature.*

*The day Kwan Yin sat on my shower wall laughing down at me was the beginning of my instruction. For the next four years, through her, I entered a period of magical teaching. I would climb into my shower and she would download stories of the magic of the universe, the meaning of reality, and an understanding of life that stays with me until today. She showed me myths, galaxies, shapes, algebra, and music. She instructed me in such multi-dimensional and painstaking detail that I had no language for it. Even today, nearly fourteen years later, I cannot entirely comprehend or share what I came to know.*

*Throughout this process, the laughing-eyed, abundant Kwan Yin would teach, chide, tease, and lead me through my instruction. She would step me into the circles of the Flower of Life, a symbolic geometrical shape represented often in nature. It is linked to the Golden Mean and sacred geometry, a symbolic way of working with change and creation in alignment with nature. I experienced the meaning and connections of the circles. I journeyed their overlaps and the shapes they made, and learned their truth was valid in all ways. My learning flung me out into the expansive eternity of the universe and I found myself floating in the same universe as my inner cells. Everything became one in pattern.*

*This was very psychedelic, but I never felt unsafe. I felt held by complete love and trusted that I was always being watched and cared for. The challenge was when I came out of these experiences and felt like a complete crazy lady. I was embarrassed to tell people what I was experiencing. I wondered if this is what happens when people are diagnosed with mental illnesses. My ego would degrade the intense beauty I was experiencing and sometimes I would come into the shower raging that, this time, I wasn't going to do this crazy stuff. Kwan Yin would laugh at me in a gentle loving way and show me this was just conditioned fear. She would guide me by answering endless questions until I felt total peace. It took me a while, but eventually I transcended all that angst.*

*During my showers, Kwan Yin would chat with me, or explain something to me, and then she would show me how to "dance" what I learned back into my life outside the shower. It was such practical, creative, inspiring truth, taught with a wonderful mix of awe and irreverence: sometimes bawdy, sometimes academic, always loving. She would tell me creation stories using archetypes, advise me on herbs or simple support medicines. I learned to use Epsom salt in the bath to clear, sugary tea to ground, and red polish on my toenails to look sexy and keep me earthy. She would show me geometric shapes, tell me what they represented, and then show me how that related to me. I learned to align my body by working with shapes like the cross, triangle, and circle.*

*I came to rely on this comfort and companionship. I would climb into the shower brimming with questions about my child, the world, philosophy, and what to do about this or that. Often, when I was stuck in my ego, she would answer my questions with wisecracks: "Oh, so you're worried you're crazy? Well, of course you are! You wouldn't be talking to a fat lady on the wall of the shower if you were sane. Mind you, where would you get better conversation right now? Rather be happy than sane!" and she would laugh so much, with everything about her wobbling, that I always knew I couldn't give up the process; there was too much about it that was just right. I was feeling strong, clear, and authentic. I knew she was teaching me truth. She would chase me with questions until I cornered myself and burst out laughing. She would hold me as I let go, let go, and let go some more. She kept me safe. She Knew. She understood, supported, and enlightened me with her answers, her humor, and her teaching.*

*I would emerge from the shower glowing, alive, and grounded in trust and knowing. My spirit would have been drawn out through the eye of my ego and I would find a crazy bliss in being who I really was. I'm sure my breast milk was enlivened with vibrational information. I believe my mothering now has its own wisdom because of what I came to know.*

*Three years after my son was born, I gave birth to my daughter and continued to receive Kwan Yin's guidance and teaching. With my son, she taught me to be authentic; with my daughter, she encouraged me to be powerful. She challenged me to expand and grow, to throw out dogma, and to free myself of fear. My lessons became less frequent, but my experiences grew more intense.*

*I re-directed my life to align with what I had learned from Kwan Yin and to put the teaching into practice. I deepened my authenticity and hunted for profound truth. Years later, my life is a completely different reality from that of my long-ago shower-mother self. Grounded in truth, and with much experience under my belt, I find myself wiser and emotionally pared down: a Woman Who Knows.*

*Sometime later, we moved from that house to a new life in a new place. I often wonder how that shower was for the next occupiers of our old house. I wonder if Kwan Yin still holds court there. I didn't see her much after our teachings completed. As all wise mothers do, she sent me off to practice what I had learned and grow into what I was to become.*

## She Appears!

*Occasionally, over the years, she has come in as I have worked with people in my coaching, mentoring, healing, and counseling. We have always had a strong bond, filled with humor and alliance. I last saw her when the house we were living in burned down: I had a moment, standing among the flames and the smoke, when I felt that I might not make it out. As I experienced my first moment of real fear, everything went calm and I felt a sea-air/ozone/water presence. With it came the absolute conviction that my family and I were safe and would be looked after. Everything ended in that moment. My life completed and a new one began. That moment, when all came to peace, carried me through the fire and out the other side of the event.*

*Since then, my spiritual experience has been less personal. Kwan Yin has become a Presence in my life, rather than a Being with form. My relationship with her is no longer a conversation, in a shower or anywhere else. I can only describe the way I experience Kwan Yin now as transcendent.*

# White-Robed, Child-Bringing Kwan Yin – Textile Art by Lydia Ruyle

Lydia Ruyle, artist, author, and scholar emerita at the University of Northern Colorado, has traveled the globe in search of sacred images of women. She has led women's pilgrimages to sacred sites, and speaks at conferences in the United States and internationally. She is also the mother of three children and grandmother of six.

The following image is one of her Goddess Icon Spirit Banners, which are sewn, collaged, and painted on nylon. These banners, the first of which she was called to create in 1995, now number 300. They have, she reports, "flown in forty countries, spreading their divine female energies."

Kwan Yin holds a child, perhaps bringing it to grateful parents. Ruyle has visited Kwan Yin's sacred island, Putuo Shan, and situates her bodhisattva on a lotus throne there. She says of the painting, "Willow grows around her reaching for water and clouds, a pure lotus flowers from the dark earth below. The Chinese characters are Kwan-yin's name: Guan Shih Yin, she who hears the cries of the world."

**White-robed, Child-bringing Kwan Yin**, Lydia Ruyle

# Whispers of My Soul – Memoir and Photograph by Lucy Keoni

Lucy Keoni, who describes herself as a "happiness coach, dream catcher, transformation catalyst, and human rights activist," comes of Vietnamese parentage. She had her first life-saving encounter with Kwan Yin in her mother's womb, in a boat on the high seas. Lucy has always felt a strong association with her mother, and has memorialized her deep connection to Kwan Yin with the splendid tattoo pictured here. Her story is one of struggle and success, always in the radiance of the bodhisattva.

Lucy writes:

*It's been said that our souls whisper our names to our parents before we enter this world. My soul whispered Nam Phuong, Phoenix from the South, the name of the last empress of Vietnam.*

*My odyssey began long before my physical birth into this world. My story begins with my mother, who grew up in a Mekong Delta town. She was married at the age of sixteen and had my older brother and sister soon after. A few years later, her husband was imprisoned for fighting on the side of the Americans, leaving her alone to provide for her young children.*

*As she struggled to take care of her family and earn enough money to buy tickets on a boat out of the country, she somehow became pregnant with me . . . a story she refuses to tell me to this day. But my soul knows: I chose my mother and father.*

*My first battle with death took place in her womb. My mother turned to Chinese herbal medicine to abort me. After three unsuccessful attempts, she finally realized that I was surely meant to be, perhaps having some special purpose in this life.*

*My mother had tried to leave Vietnam twice before. Now that she was pregnant with me, she tried again. She begged an honest fisherman to show mercy upon a pregnant woman and her two young children, and he took her onto his boat.*

*The trip was rough, the tiny boat overcrowded with people piled up on each other. They quickly ran out of water and food. Starving, thirsty, and sea-sick, my mother cried out to whatever god would save us. In the darkest hour, Kwan Yin, the Chinese Goddess of Mercy and Compassion, appeared to her from the sky, descended, and touched her plump belly, assuring her that we would reach land in the morning. Sure enough, as the darkness gave way to the breaking dawn, the boat hit a sandy beach in Malaysia.*

*Kwan Yin has saved my life over and over. I carry her on my back now. She stands tall on a lotus, spanning most of the right side of my back, down my right cheek. It took four long hours to get my patron goddess forever imprinted on my body. It was worth every agonizing rip in my skin.*

*We spent the next couple of months in a Malaysian refugee camp before being trans-ferred to the Philippines, where I arrived into this lifetime on September 30, 1981. A month later we made our way to America, sponsored by a Catholic Church in Iowa. When we arrived in what seemed an icy cold alien planet, the church baptized and named me Lucia—which means light—after St. Lucia.*

*So here I am today, a balance of Nam Phuong, Kwan Yin Divine Mother Bodhisattva, and Saint Lucia, a woman who had the courage to stand up for truth in spite of torture and death—like Kwan Yin, a purveyor of light.*

# Kwan Yin in the City – Memoir by Estrella Root

Mothers and daughters who presumably share the same lifestyle and preferences can be worlds apart in their sensibilities. Estrella Root and her daughter are both lesbians, but on a visit to her daughter, Estrella found herself distressed and assaulted by the environment in which her daughter seemed comfortable. She recounts a jarring experience of dislocation, coming from her peaceful rural home in New Mexico to a noisy apartment in San Francisco where her daughter was staying, in which she was confronted with disturbing images and chaotic, possibly dangerous surroundings. Still, out of love for her daughter, she wanted to adapt to the situation. She tells how she turned to Kwan Yin for help.

Estrella writes:

*My daughter lives abroad. I had not seen her for six years, and was anticipating a rare state-side visit with complete exhilaration. We were meeting in San Francisco for a few days, then proceeding to Mendocino, where she grew up and where we had friends and places to stay, places to relax by the ocean we both loved. The place I expected to stay in San Francisco was not available for the first two days of our city visit and my daughter's friend generously offered me her front room couch so we could be together.*

*Though my daughter and I are both lesbians, we hail from completely different parts of the culture. A gender warrior who calls herself "queer," she is oriented toward large cities, tattooed and pierced from head to foot, with a buzzed shock of brightly dyed hair. At this point, it was wheat field yellow and carmine red. I am an eco-warrior Buddhist witch, living on women's land in the Sangre de Cristos Mountains of New Mexico. I call myself a "land dyke." Believe me, many of our values are quite different.*

# She Appears!

*This was immediately apparent when we trudged up the stairs to her friend's apartment on Folsom Street downtown, a seedy neighborhood that was just starting to be trendy. The couch was at the front, where a large window overlooked a heavily trafficked street full of bars, homeless people, and drunks—a far cry from my sweet cabin in the woods! Her friend, a tattoo artist in the Castro, had covered the walls with her portraits of San Francisco queers, all in somber colors with many images of leather gear, penises, and dildos. One photograph of a naked woman and her dog seemed to suggest they were about to have sex. This was quite different from the colorful pictures of buddhas, bodhisattvas, and goddesses that adorned my home, and incredibly dismaying. With all the suffering surrounding us, how could I enjoy this reunion? I was in hell, and had to act like this was normal, good, and okay, which I did for the duration of the evening. I smiled and pretended to be fine, when in fact I was incredibly disturbed by the ugliness I saw, which these young people accepted and even seemed to admire.*

*As I lay there that night on the couch, listening to the inebriated shouting of suffering and unhappy people, I cried out to Kwan Yin. I had set up an image of her for my traveling altar beside me. As I quietly breathed in and out, I felt this warm undulating fog envelop the street and its people and the room where I had been trying to sleep. I knew it was the goddess. She had come to help, her compassion all-pervading in its warmth and love.*

*All judgment dropped from me. I saw the salacious dog picture as just a woman and her dog. It was I who had added the mental formations onto everything.*

*Without my judgments, in the days that followed, my daughter and I and her friend had a lovely time in San Francisco, and everywhere else we went, thanks to Kwan Yin's compassionate and open heart.*

# My Mother as Kwan Yin – Sculpture by Miriam Davis

Miriam Davis has been showing her ceramic, painting, and mixed media work for 25 years, and has been practicing Buddhism for nearly as long. Her first glimpse of Kwan Yin came in a picture puzzle depicting the Kwan Yin statue in Kansas City, which she sees as "elegant and gentle." She has created a number of surprising sculptures of Kwan Yin. This one she calls "My Mother as Kwan Yin," and says of it, "I enjoyed making a sort of tribute to my mother by envisioning her as an enormous figure (our mothers are gigantic presences in our lives) in a forties dress, reclining among mountains."

So Miriam has taken a leap from the Asian representations of Kwan Yin that inspire many artists, all the way across the ocean to California where she now lives, to give us her own full-bodied, red-headed mother. This Kwan Yin holds the vial of compassion in one hand and a lotus blossom in the other; her gown suggests flowing ocean water, and she dwarfs the mountains. The photograph shows the sculpture resting in backyard grass, present here with us, the way Mom is.

It prompts the question: Does Kwan Yin have to be exotic and gracefully remote, or can she reside more intimately in our own earthly, fleshly mothers, no matter how monumental, and in our own so-imperfect selves?

**My Mother as Kwan Yin,** Miriam Davis

# Two Encounters – Memoirs by Nancy Cavaretta

Nancy Cavaretta is a college instructor at Roosevelt University in Chicago, a Buddhist, and a single mother of three children. She experienced two remarkable encounters with the bodhisattva, the first before she knew anything about Kwan Yin, the second a transcendent dream vision of flying out into the universe with her. The first helped her grapple with difficult family dynamics and allowed her to function better as a mother; the second radically changed her life.

Nancy writes:

### One: Dream Invitation, February 2000

*It was a chilling winter Chicago evening, and my three children and I were preparing for bed. I recall pushing the blinds aside from the living room window to watch the heavy but peaceful accumulation of snow drift closely to the top of the fence that surrounded our home. It was a dark time for our family. I was going through a treacherous divorce and had moved from a large home to a small apartment with three children and a puppy that was going to get big. If ever there was a time when I needed the guidance, strength, and hope from a loving mother, it was then. Pushing the blinds in place to keep out the cold, I settled into bed after making sure everyone was warm and comfortable. We were all looking forward to sleeping late into the coming Saturday morning.*

*Although I was raised Catholic by Italian parents, I never could embrace their religious beliefs. At the age of nineteen, I had studied in a Theravada Buddhist temple for nine months. In this Buddhist tradition, there are no images of Divine Feminine nor is there any reference made to such a notion, yet principles of the Dharma have remained with me throughout my life path.*

*That snowy Chicago evening brought with it the comfort of deep sleep and a dear friend whom I had not seen before in this lifetime. The dream began with a large, ornate picture frame that hung on a wall. The thick frame was made of red mahogany and intricately carved. At first, no picture was present on the canvas. Shortly after viewing the frame, I heard a song begin to play at an almost uncomfortably loud volume. The song was "I Can See Clearly Now" and the lyrics declared "It's gonna be a bright, bright sunshiny day." As the song played on, a picture appeared inside the frame. It was a vivid image of green hills and pastures with a farm house embedded in a valley. The picture radiated peace. Within moments of viewing the scene, I realized it was not a picture at all, but a window looking out onto endless pastures of greenery and flowers. Trees swayed in the breeze.*

*Then came the shadow: A blackened side view of what I thought was the Buddha, sitting in a lotus position, superimposed itself upon the scene. The image started off seeming far away, but grew larger as it came closer. I remember thinking it could not be the Buddha because it was wearing a scalloped lace veil placed over an elevated headpiece. The music grew louder and finally the figure turned forward and faced me. It was an Asian woman. She was smiling and pointing to the beautiful scene behind her. She then motioned to me to come. When I reached out to her, I awakened into the morning light.*

*I was so filled with shock over what I had seen in the dream that I reviewed it in my mind many times. When the children woke up, I asked if anyone wanted to go to Chinatown. They were puzzled by my request, given the weather, and refused my offer, until I told them about the dream. I explained to them my intent to search the shops and discover the identity and meaning of the Buddha woman in my dream. Then they agreed to accompany me.*

*In Chinatown, we located several images, some of which even displayed the intricate lace edge of her head covering. A few of them were labeled with a name: Kwan Yin. At first, we had a difficult time finding shopkeepers who spoke enough English to describe her identity and role. Finally, we met with a Chinese couple who explained that she is a bodhisattva who brings compassion and aid to all, but particularly to women and children. I knew it had been Kwan Yin who had visited me in my dream.*

*This was the beginning of my journey with Kwan Yin, or at least the part I had finally become aware of. As the weeks went by, I could not let go of the images, in particular the verdant hills with their peace, harmony, and promise of relief from the gauntlet my life had become. The contrast of the present darkness and the future promise of a bright and sunshiny day had been brought to me by a version of the Divine Feminine championing the causes of women and children. In perfect synchronicity, Kwan Yin remained daily at my side. Growing up Catholic, I was no stranger to living in the presence of images that represented saints and angels. I returned to Chinatown alone two weeks after the dream in search of an image that captured the vision I held in my mind of the smiling*

*Buddha-woman garbed in a lace veil. The search led me immediately to the perfect image of Kwan Yin, which has continued to hold a prominent position in the places I've called "home."*

*More important than the presence of her image was the deep shift that took place in my confidence that the divorce proceedings would not continue to destroy me and my children. My spirit had obviously lightened, and this shift produced a more hopeful climate for us. My daily meditations brought insights informing me that I had experienced a true encounter with Kwan Yin, and through the deep reflective process of meditation, I realized she would be and always was with me. I saw her presence in the many signs and reassurances she provided for me as I opened myself to become conscious of her presence in my life. I longed to see her again and feel her presence in the sensory and matter form that human beings need to validate the presence of the spiritual. I wanted to see her again.*

### Two: An "Astral" Journey, October 31, 2001

*It was Halloween night, and my children were engaging in the traditional rite of trick-or-treat while I dispensed candy at home, accompanied by our golden retriever, who was dressed as an angel. We lived directly across the street from an elementary school and a small park. As the next morning was a school day, my daughter had friends spending the night so they could get an early start and get to school on time. That evening, I decided to sleep on the couch in the living room to get away from the giggling and read myself to sleep.*

*The divorce proceedings had now reached the third year. I was on the verge of bankruptcy. I was existing somewhere between questioning everything I had ever believed and wanting to leave the human experience behind. No place ever seemed safe. I took only the slightest crumbs of joy from the silliness of our golden retriever's antics and the small pleasures of listening to giggling preteens enjoying a sleepover. And there was always my previous encounter with Kwan Yin. Although she continued to be with me, I missed her physical presence as a child misses the hugs of a deceased mother, present in memory and spirit but absent in the world of senses and matter. As I tried to erase the spikes of anxiety that competed with my physical fatigue, the giggling helped me fall quickly asleep.*

*On this night, while asleep, I believe I actually left my body and walked across the street to my children's school. Groups of unsavory characters were hanging around the park. I had gone to the school to pick up report cards, but it was difficult to get in because of the heckling, stealing, and conning taking place on the park grounds. I finally made it into the building and was told by a teacher that I was too late to obtain the report cards and that I should go into the auditorium and wait. I was puzzled because the school did not have an auditorium, but then I turned my head to the left and saw a large wooden door. When I opened the door, there was an auditorium with wooden seats and a stage. A handful of people were sitting and waiting.*

*I then spotted a dear spiritual friend, who does not have children, sitting in the front row. She waved to me and, as I looked at her, I saw Kwan Yin sitting in a lotus position on the stage. Behind her was a blue backdrop of a hue and intensity I had never seen before. Kwan Yin was all white, as though translucent. It was obvious only my friend and I could see her. I even asked a woman near me if she could see anyone on the stage and she declined. Then my smiling friend said, "Go to her."*

*As there was no middle aisle, I climbed over the wooden seats to move toward Kwan Yin more quickly. She was beginning to levitate from the stage floor and I did not want to miss her. Finally, I reached the stage and climbed up. As she rose above my head, I grabbed her foot and immediately felt magnetism so strong that she was able to lift me up from the floor and into the air. We then passed through the roof, moving upward through the night sky.*

*I could feel the cold as we glided toward higher elevations and the wind blew her sheer white clothing against the midnight blue evening sky. Only Kwan Yin's black hair deviated from her all white appearance. Stars shone all around. It was silent and peaceful as our magnetic connection of hand-to-foot remained solid and trustworthy. We approached the moon. I could see her face in the moonlight. No words were spoken until I said, "I'm ascending." Kwan Yin replied, "You have already ascended. Now, go back." And I did, gliding down to earth.*

*In the days that followed, I spent what seemed to be endless amounts of mental time reviewing and re-visiting the barrage of sensory experiences on my journey with Kwan Yin. The reality of the cold, the magnetism from her body to mine, the burning stars against the night sky, the levitation, the elevation, the speed of descent back to earth, remained simultaneously present to me as I navigated through my daily duties and obligations. The sensory experiences all told me I had made a real journey with her. I had needed to see and feel her. She had granted my request, but there remained the question of the meaning of her words, "You have already ascended. Now go back."*

*Within months of my journey with Kwan Yin, the divorce proceedings moved into the final stages. Soon I would be free from the incessant litigation and shadow of daily uncertainty about my fate and the fate of my children. No longer did I wish for the termination of the human experience, as I felt a sense of transcendence over my circumstances. I became conscious of the fact that I needed to re-acquaint myself with the joy I once felt from my chosen field of special education. This prompted me to make some changes in what I was actually doing to improve the field. While searching out what these changes would be, I studied and meditated upon the essence of the bodhisattva and how Kwan Yin's presence in the world brings perpetual comfort and healing. I promised her that I would strive to live the precepts of the bodhisattva vow in this lifetime on Earth. A copy of this vow is present in my home and in my workplace.*

*May I be a guard for all those who are protector-less,*
*A guide for those who journey on the road.*

*For those who wish to go across the water,*
*May I be a boat, a raft, a bridge.*

*For all those ailing in the world,*
*Until their every sickness has been healed,*

*May I myself become for them*
*The doctor, nurse, the medicine itself.*

*My journey with Kwan Yin was enough to last me throughout this lifetime and beyond. I miss her physical presence no more. She is always with me.*

## Compassion – Painting by Reena Burton

While Nancy Cavaretta eloquently describes Kwan Yin as the mother, Reena Burton presents Kwan Yin as the young daughter, carrying forward the compassionate nurturance she experienced in her own childhood. Reena grew up in rural California, nurtured by "a deeply giving, loosely spiritual, and closely connected family." Service, ritual, community, and Women's Spirituality inform her life and inspire her art. Passing on the strong support she experienced as a child, she has worked for years with young people, teaching art and community building. She has studied theology and worked for a time in youth ministry, teaching young people skills to access their creative and spiritual voice. And now she has had a child of her own. Reena embodies an engagement across the generations, as daughter and mother, defining her life.

Burton's Hawaiian "Compassion" Kwan Yin has none of the costume or jewelry that mark the classical goddess, but the artist sees in her thoughtful, gentle face the expression of the bodhisattva's compassionate nature. She is an island woman, wearing tropical blossoms in her hair. She embodies the essence of the bodhisattva, the young dimension of Kwan Yin. She is the daughter, carrying on the work.

Reena says of her: "Initially I thought of Kwan Yin as a model of giving and compassion for me as I went about my work in ministry and service to others, though after burnout and eventual illness due to self-sacrifice, I learned that the best lesson Kwan Yin could teach me was to have compassion toward myself first. If I wasn't nurturing my own spirit, I could not nurture anyone else's, either. She's one of my favorite goddesses because of this lesson."

Reena participates in a cycle of nurturing: daughter in a supportive family group, sister and mentor to young people, and mother now raising her own first child. She is learning to bring Kwan Yin's caring to herself as well as to the world.

Compassion,
Reena Burton

# Mother Kannon, Womb of Compassion – Memoir by Paula Arai

Paula Arai, a Buddhist studies scholar at Louisiana State University, experienced strong affinity with Kwan Yin in the Japanese form, called Kannon, through her Japanese-born mother. She tells of three generations touched by Kannon—mother, daughter, son—in a history rooted in her Asian heritage and equally expressing her North American perspective.

Paula writes:

*Late spring wildflowers bloomed along the pilgrimage path leading to the temple in the Chichibu Mountains of Japan. Eight Japanese grandmothers looked intently upon me where I stood with my fingers wrapped around the large pumpkin-sized rock hallowed in the temple grounds. Would I join the women who, over the ages, have successfully lifted this rock straight up and thereby activated the fertile powers of Kannon-sama/Kwan Yin and ensured the conception of a healthy child? My mother, delighted to be doing this pilgrimage on her native soil with me, her half-Caucasian daughter, spearheaded a flock of wise women who knew how children really come into the world. I was 35, wanting a child, afraid my marriage would not sustain the strains of continued distance. Standing in the midst of these women, I began to realize they were teaching me that conceiving a child had more to do with preparing a nest of compassion in my heart than with trying to control the sometimes heart-wrenching logistics of a couple living on separate continents: I in America, he in China. Bearing children is women's work.*

*One of the temples along this sacred path has the most enthralling Buddhist figure I have ever beheld, a larger-than-life wood carving of Mother Kannon in sinuous robes nursing an infant at her exposed breasts, full with life-nourishing milk. The wooden prayer tablets at this temple are testimony to the streams of women who have found their way here, holding in their hearts concerns for children they longed to birth, children they hoped would study hard, children they wanted to be healthy, and children who had died. Travelling to each of the 34 temples on this popular pilgrimage route with my mother, I came to see this as a journey that weaves generations of hearts together.*

*Having managed to raise the twenty-something-pound rock four inches above the dais, I realized I had to be careful to set it down without smashing the tips of my fingers. After doing so, I took a quick, deep inhale. I had not breathed during this rite of passage into the community of women who enjoyed mothering. I was welcomed into this community with exhales of "good, good," "it is done," and giggles, not of naïve girls, but of women who knew the root cause of death is birth.*

*Redbuds were blooming that morning in Nashville when the effect of lifting Kannon's rock at that mountain temple came to fruition. After settling into the maternity ward, I called my mom from the bed at Vanderbilt University Medical Center. I was in waiting mode. My water had broken at 3 o'clock that morning. When I had arrived at the hospital, they had first wheeled me into one of the pretty rooms of the maternity ward. Then the doctor calculated I was five-and-a-half weeks early. I was quickly moved to a room with much more medical equipment on display. When I told my mom what was happening, she did not believe me. I had been a bit of a prankster when I was a child and it was April Fool's Day. Indeed, as if prescribed by his birth date, my beloved son soon revealed a buoyant and humorous spirit.*

*I began mothering on my own, because my son's father made a clear commitment to the limited contribution he could make from China. My mother flew from Detroit to Nashville to help me care for her grandson in the daytime while I finished my book manuscript for* Women Living Zen. *My editor at Oxford University Press said she had heard many late-manuscript excuses in her day, but giving premature birth was a first. When I returned from my momentous errand to the post office to mail the two-month-overdue manuscript, my mother was attaching origami fishnets and stars to a stalk of bamboo she had amazingly managed to cut down from the steep hillside. July 7 would be Kenji's first Tanabata Star Festival, which celebrates the one night of the year two ancient lovers can meet in the sky. On this auspicious night, many people believe their deepest wish, too, will be fulfilled, and my mom wanted to add her prayers for her grandson's health and well-being. Despite this, she did not display the effervescence that usually accompanies her preparations for a celebration. She admitted she did not feel well. She was not one to readily see a doctor, so I knew it was serious when she agreed to go.*

*After painful diagnostic tests and major surgery to remove fluids choking her heart, my mom's doctor recommended we focus on cherishing our time together. When he added he would get us in touch with hospice, the immediacy of his wise recommendation started working its way through us. Over the next six months, Kenji entertained us on my mother's bed, where she was ever-clad in her favorite color, purple. That is where he first sat up. Laughter rippled through us as he gleefully pulled every single tissue out of each box placed on her bed to be at hand for sudden needs. During that period when the beginning and end of life were directly in front of us, seeing what was important was never easier.*

*My mother died on December 18, 1996. It was Kannon's day. Japanese culture recognizes buddhas and bodhisattvas on a specific day of the month, and those who feel particularly close to a certain awakened figure consider it an auspicious day to do important things. To die on that day is the highest of honors. The Zen nun who comforted me stressed that my mother was now liberated to do Kannon's work, especially for her family. Kenji and I would not be left alone.*

*As he grows up, Kenji and I carry with us matching amulets of Kannon/Kwan Yin. According to a tradition of associating Japanese Buddhist figures with the Chinese zodiac, Thousand-Armed Kannon is the protective bodhisattva for both Kenji and me, since we were both born in the Year of the Rat. Though he is the son of a Buddhist scholar and has been pushed in a stroller and scampered along many paths leading to numerous urban and mountain temples, I did not know how this was shaping his orientation to the world. But on a trip to Japan when he was nine years old, we visited a temple consecrated to the Thousand-Armed Kannon, and he insisted that I buy, not one, but two fine, carved-wood amulets of Kannon. When I objected that I could really only afford one of these treasures, he reminded me that we would need two, because "Thousand-Armed Kannon protects both of us."*

*At our home altar sanctified by Kannon, every December 18, Kenji and I chant the Heart Sutra and light extra-special incense for my mother, Kenji's grandmother. As she desired, we released her ashes into the womb of the Pacific Ocean to flow freely between the lands of her birth and death.*

# Kwan Yin and the Inner Child – Painting by Mary Cutsinger

Artist Mary Cutsinger, whom I introduced in Chapter One, was the mother of five daughters. She knew a great deal about the labor and joy of child-rearing. Mary became a devotee of Kwan Yin at age 23, while raising two toddlers and with a third baby in her belly, when she encountered the famous statue in the Nelson-Atkins Museum in Kansas City. From this first glimpse onward, Kwan Yin became a source of fascination, revelation, and comfort to her, and the subject of numerous works of art. She made many images of the bodhisattva, from the most sensitive depictions of empathy with suffering, to the most lighthearted, whimsical renderings.

In this painting of Kwan Yin, accompanied by a very dressed-up child, both perched on the back of a bear, Mary is clearly having fun. It's true Kwan Yin is often shown riding a dragon and sometimes an elephant. In one striking set of ceramic statues, she sits atop each of the twelve animals of the Chinese Zodiac. (Having been born in the Year of the Rat, I am the proud possessor of a Kwan Yin mounted on a pony-sized white rat.) But I suspect Mary's is the only image of Kwan Yin riding a big brown bear.

Her title signals the humor of her perspective and connects the traditional-looking Kwan Yin with a very modern concept.

**Kwan Yin and the Inner Child**, Mary Cutsinger

# Chapter Five
# Visitations/Gradual Awakenings

She appears. This we know. And she comes in response to need, from the extremity of physical danger such as the perils undergone by the Vietnamese boat people, to the many lesser crises of our lives: the moments we are trapped in destructive patterns and need to break free, but don't know how; the moments we know everything in our lives is pressing us forward into a heightened awareness or capacity, yet we can't move. Depression, frustration, restlessness, impatience, physical pain—it is when we are in these conditions that Kwan Yin appears, and sometimes her very presence illuminates the path and points in a wholesome, new direction.

There are crucial differences in these visitations. Most dramatic is a visible human manifestation in our waking life: We encounter someone who interacts with us and, either at the time or later, we realize it was Kwan Yin. Or Kwan Yin makes herself vividly available in a dream, where she offers reassurance, sometimes through a vision of beauty and peace. Then there are the more generalized awarenesses, like a compelling sense of safety and gentle compassion for oneself and others. This may build up gradually over years until it becomes a stable part of our psyche, or it may ebb and flow with the events of our lives.

My own awareness of Kwan Yin has developed over decades. Despite my long journey to Putuo Shan and hopes for a vision there, I have never literally seen the bodhisattva appearing in traditional, recognizable form before me, but instead have had powerful experiences of knowing she was with me, surrounding and inside me. On Putuo Island, as I have described, I encountered her not as a vision but permeating the natural world and my own body; in the hospital after my cancer surgery and in the months of chemotherapy treatments, the oncology nurses and the friends who cared for me embodied Kwan Yin.

I sense her strong presence when I repeat the Chinese "Namo Guan Shih Yin Pusa" chant I learned at the City of Ten Thousand Buddhas, when I lead a Kwan Yin dance taught to me by the Sufis, and when I hear the recorded chant, "She who hears the cries of the world," by Jennifer Berezan. In the words of the South African Buddhist teacher Thanissara, "Kwan Yin is nothing but a metaphor for the responsiveness of the universe." Her practice is all about listening, hearing the cries of the world. When we listen deeply, the universe responds; we connect to our patient hearts, resting in universal awareness, returning to the energy of the Mother.

For my birthday this year, my partner gave me an exquisite Chinese ceramic statue of Kwan Yin; whenever I look at this image I feel connected to that larger consciousness. This is a lifelong relationship that I expect to last until my final breath, when, I hope, as Berezan sings, "she carries me to the other side." The other side, which is reachable right now, means the condition of utter equanimity and spaciousness that we call enlightenment and that everyone accesses now and then; but it can also mean the inevitable destination, death.

The women and one man in this section give evidence of the many ways to know Kwan Yin. Whether through direct visual contact or a felt sense of presence, whether occurring in one moment or recurring over time, these encounters served to open the recipient to a more spacious view or a more compassionate and realistic understanding of one's own predicament. As illustrated in the following story, Kwan Yin often arrives when she is most needed.

## The Lady in the Dark – Memoir by Florence Caplow

Florence Caplow is a Zen priest, botanist, essayist, and editor of several books. Her anthology, *The Hidden Lamp*, co-edited with Susan Moon, collects stories from 25 centuries of enlightened women. In her rovings as an itinerant monk, teacher, and seminarian, she has learned that Kwan Yin's aid and comfort do not appear only when called upon, but exist perpetually in our environment, in our hearts, in those around us. We need only "notice," she says, in order to find them where they wait "with a deep and inexhaustible patience" for us.

Caplow tells of a late-night, mysterious encounter at a meditation center that helped her break out of an existential impasse. She reports the internal dialog we often have in these circumstances when our rational 21st-century minds seek to dilute or deny what we saw or felt while our deeper nature gently insists upon what it experienced. Caplow's middle-of-the-night encounter opened and informed her, one of the many influences that led to her eventual ordination as a Zen priest and the acceptance of her calling.

Florence writes:

*It is early spring at the Spirit Rock Meditation Center in Northern California, and I am near the end of two months of silence and meditation. Although I have been a student of both Zen and vipassana for many years, this is the longest time I've been in silent retreat. I have deepened until everything is transparent, like a clear mountain lake. From this subtle and slowed-down state, I've seen how suffering starts in every moment with a lean into the next moment, a desire for the next moment, and how stuck I am in that lean. It feels like there is nothing more important in the world than to be free from identifying myself with "that which leans into the next moment." For days, I have felt right at the edge of understanding, but unable to walk through to the other side.*

*It's raining, as it has been for the last month, and it's late, long after most people have gone to sleep. I go for a walk in the rain and the dark, carrying my dilemma with me. The rain beats on my umbrella, on the branches of the bay laurels bent down and glistening, on the dried grasses on the hill. Mud runs in rivulets across the road. On the way back to my room I walk past the Spirit Rock "gratitude hut": a small octagonal building, less than ten feet across, with photos and quotes from the great Buddhist teachers of the 20th century. For weeks I've been taking care of the hut, sweeping it, and keeping it clean, inspired by all the wisdom represented there in those simple black-and-white photos. I decide to go inside.*

*I open the wooden door and close it behind me to keep out the rain. I can hear the water from my umbrella dripping on the floor, and it is black as a moonless midnight inside the hut. It's spooky to stand in total darkness with the rain thundering on the roof, and it doesn't feel like the same sweet place I swept out earlier in the day.*

*I stand in front of the altar with my hands together, but the darkness is so absolute that I could be anywhere. I ask for help, silently, but with all my heart. Help me to move beyond my narrow view, help me to wake up, help me to know the truth of my life. Half consciously, I notice a slight glow to my right, near one of the benches along the wall. I continue to stand with my silent prayer, I don't know for how long, but likely many minutes. Then I turn back to the door and open it to the rain.*

*There's a streetlight outside, and as I open the door, its light shines in and across the hut. I notice something out of the corner of my eye. I half-turn, and there, sitting quietly on the bench, is a small, ordinary-looking Asian woman, about my age, with long braids.*

*I am utterly shocked and startled. How could we have both been in that tiny space for so long? Why didn't she say anything? How strange must it have been for her to hear me come in, and then for me to stand there for so long? I whisper, "Sorry, I didn't see you," and flee, my heart beating wildly.*

*I walk up the hill toward my room, oblivious to the rain, trying to make sense of what has just happened. I realize she would have also been visible when I opened the door to enter the hut, and yet I had seen no one. I remember the glow to my right as I prayed for help. My mind had split. One side, the supposedly rational side, thought it must have been one of the Asian women on retreat here; no one from outside the retreat center would have been in that hut so late at night in the rain. There are three Asian women here, I thought, deciding to ask and apologize when the retreat was over. But I couldn't imagine how any human being could have stayed utterly still in total darkness, not even the sound of breath, while another person stood less than three feet away, almost close enough to touch.*

*The other side of my mind said, You nitwit! That was no fellow retreatant in there, or even if it was, this wasn't an ordinary encounter. That was Kwan Yin. You met a goddess in the gratitude hut, and all you could do was say, "I'm sorry" and run away.*

*When I got back to my reassuringly calm and ordinary room, I found a blank piece of paper and a pen. I was trembling, as perhaps people have always trembled after an encounter with something unfathomable. I drew all the symbols of Kwan Yin I knew: the moon, a willow branch, the vase with which she pours healing waters on the world. I propped the piece of paper up on my altar and did three full bows, apologizing for not recognizing her and thanking her for hearing my call for help. Meanwhile, one side of my mind was nattering about how foolish I'd feel when I found out it was one of the people at this retreat . . .*

*After the encounter in the gratitude hut, I kept Kwan Yin close to my heart, and I brought the compassionate view of Kwan Yin to my question, this koan: Why, since I truly believed my holding on to the "self that leans into the next moment" was an illusion, did that illusion feel so real and permanent? One morning, two days later, as I sat with my fellow retreatants and waited for the leader to strike the big bell to end the meditation period, a phrase arose in my mind: In this whole*

96

*world, there is not even a grain of sand to hold on to. With that, my whole story about who I was and what I was holding on to just fell apart. If I could have gotten up and danced with joy at that moment, I would have. I understood, in my very cells, that whatever I thought, whatever I believed, whatever I was sure I was holding on to, the truth was that nothing whatsoever could be held on to. It was all fine, whether I knew it or not. But at that moment, I did know it, and I was free.*

*All retreat experiences and insights are subject to fading and impermanence, just like everything else, but since that moment, even years later, an inner knowing subtly permeates my everyday experience. Every morning for the sixty days of that silent retreat, I went up on the hillside above the retreat center and watched the sunrise. Sometimes the sky was piercingly clear and blue, and the sun bounded up like a big, yellow, happy ball. Sometimes the sky was mysterious and misty, and the sun gently appeared out of the clouds. Sometimes the clouds turned every shade of pink and purple. And sometimes there was nothing to see at all, just a blank gray sky, growing imperceptibly lighter, or rain slanting down. But I always knew the sunrise was there, behind the clouds, whether I could see it or not. It has been the same with my understanding of that morning, as I sat waiting for the big bell to ring . . . I would forget, it would become a story . . . but not entirely. The sun of reality is still shining, no matter how thick the clouds of confusion that obscure it.*

*At the end of the retreat, when we were no longer in silence, I asked each of the Asian women in the retreat if they had been in the gratitude hut that rainy night. Each looked at me oddly and said "No."*

*I'm left with the unexplainable gift.*

### Postscript

*A year after the retreat, I became ordained as a Soto Zen priest on an island in Puget Sound. The eight-year-old daughter of a friend came to the ordination ceremony. When she was six, I had been with her and her parents as she lay in Children's Hospital in Seattle, desperately sick with a rare illness, deep in a medically induced coma, her mother wild with fear. I had done many services on her behalf, calling on Kwan Yin to help her. Now, here she was, healthy again, but mysteriously mature, in the way of a child who has come close to death. During the ceremony, she ran outside for a few minutes, into the late afternoon sunlight. At the end of the ceremony, she shyly presented me with a gift, a poem she had written under the weeping willow outside:*

*The willow is praying under the oak tree,*
*the willow is praying under the oak tree.*
*I pray with the willow tree,*
*the willow is always praying with me.*

*Kwan Yin carries a willow branch.*

*The next morning, I woke up very early and put on "Buddha's robe," the black Zen robe I had spent years sewing in preparation for this ordination. As I walked along the shoreline overlooking the great tidal flats of Samish Bay, I thought, This is it. This is the job I've always been called to, to be the hands and feet and eyes and ears of Kwan Yin. This is where I truly belong, finally.*

*I suspect that the great forces of compassion of the world, personified as Mother Mary or Kwan Yin, do not actually come when we call them; they're here all the time, hidden, waiting with a deep and inexhaustible patience for us. They're hidden all around us, and also within us. It is up to us to notice, whether in the desperate call for help, in the eyes of an eight-year-old child, or in our own great hearts.*

*Many bows to the Lady in the dark.*

## Listening to Kwan Yin – Painting by Marilyn Lastra–McGinley

Marilyn Lastra-McGinley, a New Jersey wife, mother, grandmother, and retired office worker, is new to painting and to Kwan Yin. She takes art classes online, and has realized she loves painting with acrylic on cardboard. In the last few years, she has become aware of the Divine Feminine. "It was then that I felt Kwan Yin drawing me into her heart," she says. Although of Catholic background and strongly connected to the Virgin Mary, Marilyn calls upon Kwan Yin for guidance and protection.

Following the inspiration of the bodhisattva's steadfast caring, Marilyn volunteers at a safe home for women who have been victims of human trafficking. She dreams of going back to the town where she was raised and starting a "community center for women of all cultures" to pass on what she has learned in her life and art-making. She sees this as "a place for women (especially lower-income, struggling women) to come, kick off their shoes to relax, take a break, and create for free."

During prayer and meditation, she asked Kwan Yin to give her an image to paint that would be "directly from the bodhisattva's heart to my own." As she watched, Marilyn says, "I saw a clear picture of her emerging from the background, first as an outline, a woman with her hands together as if praying, and then becoming more detailed, all the way to the finished image just as you see it here." She chose to put this vision on a piece of rough cardboard to "show a side of Kwan Yin that is simple, beautiful, and yet powerful and full of Divine energy." She calls it "Listening to Kwan Yin" because "She pours good energy into my heart after a long day when I was in complete stress mode at times. All one has to do is quiet their inner being and listen to what Kwan Yin has to say."

**Listening to Kwan Yin**,
Marilyn Lastra-McGinley

# Kwan Yin Visitation – Memoir by Jacqueline Gautier

Jacqueline Gautier, a Canadian in her late forties, left her home and family behind to study in the United States. Here, without her usual support, she experienced herself as ungrounded and anxious. Through a powerful dream encounter with Kwan Yin, Jacqueline found her equilibrium, and then began encountering the embodiment of the bodhisattva in random women she met in daily life. Her search for a statue of Kwan Yin led her to a very special store, Spirit Matters, where she acquired a snow-white statue of Kwan Yin to place at the center of the altar she created.

Now, ten years later, Jacqueline lives on Vancouver Island, where she works as a Registered Clinical Counselor, and remembers Kwan Yin as the companion and guide she so desperately needed.

Jacqueline writes:

*In 2003, I moved to San Francisco to undertake my master's degree in clinical psychology at the California Institute of Integral Studies. While I was very excited to begin this new chapter of my life, it represented a tremendous leap of faith and transition. At the age of 48, I sold our family home of 23 years in Saskatoon, Saskatchewan, and most of my belongings, to finance my studies. I was leaving my beautiful country, Canada, my four dear adult sons, and all my friends and family, for a period of three years. And most sadly, I was leaving my firstborn grandchild, Maia, who was graciously born two weeks early so I could hold her and tell her I loved her before departing for the United States. It was a bittersweet farewell.*

*During the first few months in the academic program, I experienced culture shock, homesickness, fear of failure, and most especially sadness in missing my new granddaughter. All these emotions rumbled just beneath the surface, as I was busy trying to keep up with my schoolwork and put on a happy face with my housemates and classmates. Most of my classmates were between the ages of 25 and 32, but I was determined not to let my age affect my ability to fit in and learn the material. On the exterior, it looked like I was managing, but inside I was in turmoil. I was afraid that if I let down my guard and started to express my true feelings, I would destabilize completely.*

*I was enrolled in the Expressive Arts Therapy program, in which there was a requirement that we undertake 75 hours of expressive arts therapy ourselves. I chose a lovely therapist by the name of Jo Sopko. The first time I visited her home office, I saw a large statue of Kwan Yin in the living room. I asked her who that was and she explained to me that this was the Asian goddess of compassion.*

*During my second session with Jo, I let down my defenses and the emotions began to pour out. She made it safe for me to trust her; I thought she embodied the goddess's energy of compassion as I told her how hard it had been for me to leave my newborn granddaughter in Canada, as well as my children, my house, my mother, my friends, everything I knew. I told her how scared and sad I was. I cried so hard, I had to lie down from the exhaustion of sobbing. I was afraid I would never stop crying, but eventually I did. When I quieted down, Jo made me tea and handed me a small ball of soft, white clay. She invited me to close my eyes and see what shape emerged from working the clay. After a few minutes, I was surprised to see I had made the form of a woman with a very large lap. It was perfect. To this day, I still have that little sculpture on my desk. Not only did I feel a tremendous sense of release during that counseling session, I sensed I had also been exposed to something very special. Little did I know what awaited me that night!*

*I went to bed that evening feeling calmer than I had for months. It was as though I had been cleansed emotionally and recalibrated. I fell asleep quickly. In the middle of the night I woke up to a very bright light in my room. I was frightened at first and didn't know what to make of it. As I propped myself up in my bed, I saw in the luminous light the form of Kwan Yin. She was very large and the purest white I had ever seen. She did not speak in words, but brought a message of compassion. She wanted me to know I was loved, her presence was near to help me, and I had nothing to fear. I basked in her luminescence for a while, feeling truly blessed. Eventually, the light diminished and I lay back down. It was impossible for me to return to sleep, as I was filled with wonder and peace.*

*After that night, everything changed. Most interestingly, over the next few weeks, I encountered Kwan Yin's presence manifested in many women. They appeared in the most random ways: on busses, at subway stations, giving me free tickets, smiling at me, loving me, hugging me, handing me their babies to hold, saying kind things to me. Her compassion was with me daily.*

*When I next saw Jo, I told her of the visitation and asked her where I could get a statue of Kwan Yin, as I felt compelled to create an altar to her. She mentioned a specialty store in a small town* called *Inverness Park* in the North Bay area. A week or so later, I decided to drive there to buy my Kwan Yin. After driving around in circles on country back roads for several hours, I was thoroughly lost. I finally stopped in a town to ask for help. Parking on the main street, I walked into a ladies' clothing shop and asked the owner to direct me to Inverness Park and to this particular specialty shop called Spirit Matters. Another woman, who was standing close by, looked at me kindly and said, "I was just going to drive there myself, why don't you follow me?" I couldn't believe this; it seemed impossible. She got in her car, and I followed her to the tiny town of Inverness Park.

At Spirit Matters, I chose a beautiful white porcelain statue about twelve inches tall. She holds a small jug in one hand and is pouring down toward the dragon at her feet, whose mouth is wide open to receive the fluid. When I paid for the statue, the saleswoman mentioned this particular statue was unique in that it had a small opening at the back where I could pour water so the vase would slowly drip, drip, into the dragon's mouth. I was delighted. The water dripping symbolized for me Kwan Yin's tears of compassion.

Eventually, I moved back to Canada and now live on beautiful Vancouver Island. I have a thriving counseling practice and beautiful new home, and my granddaughter, Maia, comes to visit often. I have experienced such abundance. My time in San Francisco was transformational. As Kwan Yin continued to express compassion to me, my heart opened and I was able to receive her loving energy, integrate it, and extend it toward others. As self-love grows, judgment and criticism diminish; we soften toward ourselves and others through Kwan Yin's loving eyes.

The Kwan Yin statue and altar are now in my office, close by where I see my clients. Her presence is a constant companion in my life and a reminder of the sacredness of the work we do "together."

# Our Lady of Compassion – Sculpture by Pamala Bird

We tend to expect Kwan Yin sightings to occur on the West or East coasts, where unconventional ideas are more readily accepted and experimentation in beliefs and lifestyles is tolerated. But as I have described, I first met Kwan Yin in Kansas City, and others have sent me their stories from the Midwest and the South of this country. Then I learned that in the rugged landscape of Mormon-dominated Utah, Kwan Yin had chosen to appear.

**Our Lady of Compassion,** Pamala Bird

Pamala Bird, who lives in Southern Utah, tells about the vision that inspired her bas relief sculpture of "Our Lady of Compassion." It was the only vision that this mother, grandmother, sculptor, painter, and retired graphic designer has ever experienced. As a Buddhist meditator, she often creates visualizations, but these are deliberate actions. Her visualization of Kwan Yin, by contrast, "was a total surprise from somewhere deep and sacred that I'm not usually able to access."

"I was meditating with 'Om Mane Padme Hum' [a Buddhist chant]," she says, "and visualizing a lotus in my heart opening up to reveal the shining jewel of compassion and its light. Suddenly, the white light from the jewel came out and hovered in front of me in the form of Kwan Yin. She placed her hand on my heart, and the light extended down through my lower body and up to the crown of my head. I was filled with light. It didn't last very long, but it was beautiful and very special for me."

Pamala's relief sculpture of Kwan Yin with accompanying dragons in their distinctively Chinese shape captures this visitation. Kwan Yin in her peaceful inwardness pours out compassion over the roiling waters of birth, old age, sickness, and death; the dragons surround her with their vivid life-energy.

# Two Encounters – Memoirs by Fred Kahn

Fourteen years ago, after Fred Kahn read a piece I'd written for a magazine, he emailed me to say that he has a "personal relationship with Kwan Yin." He sent me two brief stories. As a child he was touched by Kwan Yin in a tender, heart-opening fashion. As an adult, he became a yoga teacher, and in one of his classes he encountered a Vietnam veteran who told him the second story—of Kwan Yin's appearance and actions in a war zone. Kahn's relationship with Kwan Yin continues to inform him as he practices and teaches a form of yoga called "compassion yoga."

Fred writes:

### One: Finding My Teacher

*As a child, I had a recurring dream. I found myself in a garden, with a beautiful lady. In her hand, she held a pink flame. When she reached out to touch the center of my chest with it, the flame went inside me. I felt warm, filled with peace, love, and compassion, without having any idea who this beautiful lady was.*

*I asked my grandmother about this. (She was a Theosophist and knew about these things.) My grandmother explained the system of life-force centers in the body, and let me know that the lady had been touching an energy point in my chest. But she would not tell me who the lady was. "That you will have to find out for yourself," she said.*

*Years later, I was in a Chinese market and I saw a statue. She was the beautiful lady of my dream! I found out this statue represented the bodhisattva of compassion, Kwan Yin. For several years, I looked for material about her, but most of what I ran into was channeled material, which I distrusted, because I wasn't sure of the source. Then circumstances introduced me to a man named John Blofeld, who had written the first Western book on Kwan Yin. [Bodhisattva of Compassion: The Mystical Tradition of Kwan Yin, 1977]. Because I was intrigued by the book, I attended a weekend workshop Blofeld was leading. He became my first spiritual teacher, and I began practicing what he taught. It's called compassion yoga, and it combines Buddhism with the ancient Hindu practice of bhakti (devotional) yoga.*

### Two: Saved by Kwan Yin

*While I was preparing to lead a compassion yoga workshop, a woman called to say she was coming to the workshop with her husband, but that he was not really spiritual and might be quite negative toward what we would be doing. The couple came to the workshop, and the husband sat looking bored.*

*But suddenly, when I was showing some slides, one of them an image of Kwan Yin, he sat upright and began to cry. The wife looked sideways at him in shock, and I didn't know what was going on.*

*After the workshop, the husband said he had to talk to me. Here is what he told me.*

*"While I was in Vietnam, I got lost behind enemy lines. Suddenly out of nowhere this young woman appeared and gestured for me to follow her. At first, I wasn't sure if I should trust her, but there was something about her that was very unusual and made me lower my guard. She waved for me to walk behind her, as she led me through the underbrush to a cave. I hid inside it and remained there all night. Next morning came. The woman had disappeared. Later that day I found my way back to my unit.*

*"All these years I thought she was an Oriental version of Mary. But one of the slides you showed, [the slide] of Kwan Yin, was her!"*

# Lights Out – Memoir by Doti Boon

Doti Boon is founder and pastor of a spiritual/metaphysical community in San Jose, California. Her church, called the Center for Creative Living, draws not only gay, lesbian, and transgender members but also Christians, Native Americans, Druids, Buddhists, and Hindus. Mother of two and grandmother of seven, Doti is a person of seemingly limitless energy. She reports, "I had a fantastic seventy-fifth birthday celebration, and Corky [her partner of thirty years] proposed to me on my actual birthday. Who says it's too late to get engaged!"

In the sanctuary of her multi-faith church, housed in an office space in a mall, Doti welcomes icons and flags of all the various religions. Members of her congregation often bring in statues of deities, pictures of spiritual beings and some objects that one might consider gewgaws. She tells about a remarkable experience she had with one of the objects brought to the church: a glow-in-the-dark, green-resin-molded statue of Kwan Yin.

Doti writes:

*The color of the Kwan Yin statue is a vibrant neon-green, the look on her face is orgasmic, and she had obviously been poured from a very uneven mold, since she lists to one side. Usually she sits comfortably in our hall closet here in the church.*

*But last Mother's Day, I decided to bring out all the feminine faces of God to put in the sanctuary. Our small altar contained a painting depicting the Virgin Mary, a beautiful image of a feminine Buddha, a dynamic hand-painted statue from Mexico of Pacha Mama, and plenty of goddesses, including Isis, Aphrodite, Gaia, and many more. There, in the center, I placed our listing Kwan Yin.*

*After our Mother's Day celebration, I carefully put all of the various articles away, excluding Kwan Yin because she had to be handled very carefully so as not to topple over.*

*As I came back to get her from the altar, the lights went out in the sanctuary. Since our church is in an industrial building, when the lights go out it is extremely dark. And since I don't do well in complete darkness, I started to panic. I struggled to breathe, and my heart began banging heavily in my chest.*

*Then I noticed a small light coming from the altar, and saw it grow larger in the darkness. The glow from Kwan Yin became bigger and bigger. It was shining so brightly I could see to light candles and move about the room. During these moments, the sound of soft music emanated from the statue. My panic subsided and I picked her up and held her gratefully.*

*Now, our wonderful neon-green statue of Kwan Yin stands proudly on our altar, appreciated perhaps even more than our symmetrical goddesses.*

## All Prayers are Answered – Painting by Maya Telford

Maya Telford, a Canadian, has been an artist from an early age, working in many media. Recently she has begun to paint "soul portraits," expressing the essence of a person through visual representation.

Maya has known for many years she had two spirit companions: Kwan Yin and a Chinese goddess named Soo Chee (Tzu Chi). She recounts a striking experience with these two:

"In the early eighties, I was lying in bed meditating one night before sleep. My then-husband was already asleep next to me. As I went deep into my meditation, Kwan Yin and Soo Chee came into my vision. They motioned for me to join them; they were in a garden. I went toward them and they included me in their conversation.

"All of a sudden, I could hear my husband yelling at me, which brought me back abruptly out of my meditation. He said I was speaking Chinese. I am Anglo-Saxon and have no conscious knowledge of the Chinese language."

The following image, which Telford calls "All Prayers Are Answered" depicts the Kwan Yin of her dream surrounded by lotus petals, asleep or deep in meditation, perhaps expressing the truth that in the most profound relaxation and surrender, we touch the essence of Kwan Yin's expansive presence.

**All Prayers Are Answered,**
Maya Telford

# A Small Margin of Safety – Memoir by Kate Lila Wheeler

Novelist and short-story writer Kate Lila Wheeler, who is also a Buddhist teacher, grew up in South America and lives in Massachusetts with her husband. She tells of a difficult period in her writing life, when a subtle intervention by a "brown and plasticky" representation of Kwan Yin brought some acceptance and love.

Wheeler describes a too-familiar condition of vague dissatisfaction and frustration that many of us experience often, and tells how, unexpectedly, she was offered a delicate release. Such small gifts of the bodhisattva often pass through without being noticed or marked. But Wheeler recognized and opened herself to this healing moment. Skeptic that she is, she tempers her enthusiasm, but finally allows for an enhanced capacity to trust Kwan Yin and love herself.

Kate Lila writes:

*I bought a small resin statue of Kwan Yin last March as a souvenir and reward after a difficult teaching job. I thought I could take her home, where she might aid me in writing. My second novel was going slowly and, although I understood slowness was my process, necessary for richness and texture, I also struggled with the easy pull of distraction, the needs of others, money-making, and all my own disorganized priorities. This Kwan Yin was holding a traditional loose-leaf book and I believed the image of her as an intellectual woman would be supportive.*

*I put her on top of my computer. For some months, she sat there looking brown and plasticky, and I berated myself for spending money on an idolatrous hunk of inert matter. Any clear-your-clutter manual would have instructed me to get rid of her. (She's not the only such presence on my desk). But how do you get rid of a goddess? I moved her from the top of my computer disk drive onto one of the small audio speakers. One day she toppled off the speaker, the top of which is slightly slanted, as if to prove that I didn't care for her. I put her instead on top of a stack of cut paper I use for writing down phone messages, and basically stopped looking at her.*

*Over the course of this past year, I discovered that my sense of internal chaos and futility had less to do with inefficiency than with not caring for myself. But it wasn't really clear. Sometime in January, I remember telling a friend on the phone that my inner life was difficult, and puzzling, that I felt stuck and confused, full of despair, futility, and self-hatred. I was attempting to turn a corner, yet I wasn't sure what it was or how to do it.*

*Kwan Yin sits right next to the phone. When I hung up after that conversation, my gaze was invaded, penetrated by invisible rays of softness and goodness that seemed to be coming out of the image, but were actually part of "me." The coagulated glob of emotions I'd just raised to the surface seemed surrounded by a small margin of safety, tolerance, and love, an indefinable smoothness that allowed them to feel manageable or digestible. My initial reaction, had it been verbal, would have been, What the heck? This was a palpable, living energy, and it was definitely connected with the statue. All this coming from a plastic statue? A statue I bought in a store? I stared at Kwan Yin, sure that the feeling would reveal itself as an illusion, but it didn't go away. A subtle, transparent energy seemed to be circulating around my heart, telling me my problems weren't completely real. Who are you? was my next, unvoiced interrogation. Kwan Yin smiled her tiny, fixed smirk, her gaze modestly downcast as usual.*

*Moments later, the experience dissolved, but I had absorbed the information into my heart, and it is here again as I recall it for this writing.*

*I can't say I look at the little amber-colored statue every day. In part, that's because I'm still habitually busy and distracted. I don't want to reduce Kwan Yin to a talisman, either, asking for her intervention too often; I trust she'll be there spontaneously when I need her. But I've also begun to feel I can rely on a modicum of love for myself. It was a weird moment; as I write this little story, I'm looking at the statue again. This time it's the watery flow of her robes that catches my eye, and tells me it's better not to expect a final answer.*

# Compassion Breathes – Memoir by Diane Musho Hamilton

Diane Musho Hamilton is a spiritual teacher trained in Zen and Integral Spirituality, who offers guidance in how to transcend our limited view of ourselves and discover our own unique expression of love, wisdom, and compassion. Like Pamala Bird she lives in Utah, and describes a gentle summer evening among mountain foothills in which a group of somewhat alienated friends have a unique experience of Kwan Yin's living, breathing presence and come to peace with each other. As in Kate Wheeler's recognition of the energy coming from Kwan Yin, this was a moment that could have been missed or discounted but was acknowledged by each of the women, an instance of Kwan Yin's quiet presence in our lives when we are able to recognize her.

Diane writes:

*Jeri and I hadn't spoken for a year. It had been a classic girlfriend falling out. She had moved away from Utah to the Northwest, and we weren't connecting by phone very often. I was working a new job that demanded my attention, and I was probably less available than I had been.*

*She had become much closer to Randee, a mutual friend of ours, through their frequent phone calls. This resulted in a bit of jealousy and awkward triangulation, as well as some misunderstanding. Matters were complicated by the fact that Jeri had a new boyfriend, and I couldn't make sense of him.*

*Finally, add a dose of friendship fatigue that sets in over ten or fifteen years, and there you have it: the perfect recipe for a falling out. I guess something needed to shift between us, and when we couldn't find a way to talk it through, we just quit talking. Maybe you have been through something similar. Although no one was really to blame, at the time it felt to me like Jeri was at fault.*

*Suddenly, after a year of not speaking, she was back in Salt Lake City for the weekend. She called me on the phone and said, "Let's put up the dogs and have a drink."*

# She Appears!

*"Well, ah, yeah sure, of course," I said. Her invitations were always hard to resist; I loved her unconventional approach to things. But after I hung up, I experienced a rush of hurt and vulnerability that I couldn't sort through. I wanted to get together, but at the same time, I didn't want to touch back into the pain. I assumed it would be awkward between us, and when I tried to imagine talking over the past year, my mind quit. There was no sense in trying to go over it or talk it through. So I sat there bewildered. What do I do?*

*I looked over at the large statue of Kanzeon/Kwan Yin Bodhisattva sitting on my dresser. She is about two feet high, sitting in the leg-up posture of royal ease. She is at home in herself. At the same time, her spine is straight, and so is her gaze. She is present to all that is, while deeply awake to that which is beyond form.*

*I had given my Kanzeon a large feather to hold in one hand, and a beaded medicine bag to wear. I had also placed a small ceramic owl on one of her shoulders because of my love of birds. Her face is serene, but her gaze is penetrating. She is fearless. She rides a dragon, after all, and sometimes she brandishes swords and shields. She is completely, undeniably awake.*

*Having been raised in a secular household without the benefit of goddesses, I was slow to appreciate Kanzeon/Kwan Yin's presence in the Buddhist tradition. Gradually, I began to notice her gracing the altars of Zen temples in which I practiced. I learned she is called Kanzeon in Zen environments, and became curious when we chanted to her at the end of each Zen service. Over time, I came to fully accept her as the symbol of our potential for an awakened heart.*

*I had never made a request to a goddess before, since I only related to them as symbols. But suddenly, looking at her on my dresser, I spoke to her. "I am just going to give this evening to you, Kanzeon, because I don't know how to navigate my conflicting feelings, and I know you are wise in the ways of these things."*

*I sprang up, inspired to bring the two-foot statue outside to the garden. I placed a woven piece of Guatemalan fabric in the middle of a small patio table, and then set her on top of it. Then I put six or seven glass votive candles in front of her and lit each one. By now my anxiety was gone, and I was in a mood of complete aesthetic enjoyment. I went back inside to get a bottle of wine and glasses, flowers, and a plate of fresh peaches, cucumbers, and tomatoes for my guests.*

*In the meantime, Randee, the other member of this complicated triangle, called. She knew Jeri was in town and that we were getting together. She wanted to come over. I thought to myself, "No way. I can handle one of them, but together, these girls are too much." I paused, and again my mind seemed to fall off a shelf. I couldn't say yes, and I couldn't say no. So I said, "All right."*

*Soon after, Amy, another friend whom I hadn't seen for months and months, called. It was strange that she contacted me that same evening. A few years before, we had socialized often, but since she had left for medical school, I hadn't seen her for some time. When she heard the others were on their way, she said she was coming, too.*

*A little while later, she was walking up the winding steps to my front door in the mellowing golden light of a Utah summer evening, looking like a living goddess with her dark skin, broad bare shoulders, and sensual hips wrapped in a summer sarong. I welcomed her in.*

*All four of us were sitting outside in my small, enclosed garden, sipping wine together. Jeri was tenderly fingering the pages of a large book of photos of Edward Curtis' Native American portraits, dove-cooing over their sepia beauty. Randee held a pocket mirror up to her face, smiling as she outlined her sculpted lips in her favorite matte red lipstick. Amy sat happily in summer sandals with painted bronze toenails, and Kanzeon was silent, gracing us with her inert, yet confident presence. All was right with the world. We sat with her, and laughed like old times.*

*After about 45 minutes of our making small talk like a covey of bubbling quail, Randee turned to me with an unusual look, simultaneously open and apprehensive. "Do you see what I see?" Instead of looking at her, I glanced toward the bodhisattva, and then looked back at Randee. "Yes," I said, "I see."*

*But in fact, I wasn't at all certain what I was seeing. The statue of Kanzeon was breathing. It was one of those strange, miraculous moments people report, such as the appearance of the Virgin Mary in a tree, weeping.*

*I looked to Jeri to see if she was seeing the same thing. She nodded. And then to Amy. She, too, nodded her head. All four of us sat in poignant silence watching the statue breathing in front of us, her bronze chest rising and falling in a deep, steady rhythm, a rhythm that neither disappeared nor diminished as we looked on, rapt and wordless.*

*None of us spoke. We just sat quietly gazing at Kanzeon. Gradually, we resumed our conversation, although softly. For an inexplicable reason, not one of us was inclined to comment or question the miracle. What could we possibly say?*

*The goddess of compassion continued to breathe in and out for another two hours as the pale evening light faded to a starry sky. Finally, we stood up and wandered off together into the foothills, walking barefoot in the dark of that summer night. When we returned an hour or so later, the statue had once again become still. She has never breathed since. That is to say, the statue has never breathed again as far as I know, but I feel the cool breeze of Kanzeon's compassion every day of my life.*

# First of Three Kwan Yins – Drawing by Shoshanah Dubiner

Imagine this: a low stage backed by draperies. To the side, on the floor, sits a female musician playing a harmonium and chanting the classic Buddhist syllables with a strong resonant voice: "Om Mani Padme Hum."

At the center of the stage is a six-foot-high piece of paper. Artist Shoshanah Dubiner, wearing a long white dress, stands before this pristine snowy expanse. In her left hand she holds a small pot of black ink. In her right hand is an artist's brush.

Shoshanah raises her brush, and a bent leg takes shape on the paper. Then an arm balanced on its knee. Next come shoulders.

The chant carries us along on a river of sound as we watch the artist working with seeming ease, her body and arm creating a dance as the figure of the seated Kwan Yin emerges on the paper.

The brush brings into existence the rock she's sitting on, the roiling waves crashing against its smooth dark surface.

Now the artist paints the drapes and folds of costume, and then the facial features come into being, eyes looking downward, mouth gently curved in a smile.

Shoshanah adds the long ears that distinguish a sacred being, and she draws in the hair and the towering top knot.

Bracelets, and toes and fingers arrive on the paper. This Kwan Yin, while technically seated, could be dancing, her body and head mirroring the lively movement of the ocean water at her feet.

The artist is finished. The musician brings her chant to a climax.

Shoshanah steps aside to allow her creation to be fully visible. The audience bursts into delighted applause.

What I have evoked is a performance piece offered to a San Francisco Buddhist audience. The image you see here is one of the practice drawings Shoshanah Dubiner made to prepare for this performance. She made a number of four foot and two foot drawings to accustom her eye and hand to creating the shapes so that she would not need to sketch the image first for her larger version but could simply "dance the brush onto the paper."

Indeed that was the impression she gave as she used her brush to persuade the image and spirit of Kwan Yin to come forth. This was a visitation: as the blithe energy of her contours took shape beneath the artist's brush, the bodhisattva herself appeared before us.

**First of Three Kwan Yins**, Shoshanah Dubiner

# Invitation to Dance – Memoir by Sherry Ruth Anderson

Kwan Yin as danced, Kwan Yin as dancer. In the Hindu tradition, the goddesses are often shown dancing, their many arms brandishing implements, sometimes weapons, their feet trampling animals and human beings. In the Tibetan tradition of Buddhism, there are *yoginis* (female wisdom beings) who dance sedately or wildly. Pre-eminent among them is the buxom, sinewy Vajra Yogini whose nearly naked dancing body flashes with life.

In contrast, Kwan Yin is pictured in repose, standing or sitting, her form projecting a deep tranquility and inward-looking power even in the midst of surrounding chaos. However, Kwan Yin is not limited to her conventional renderings. After all, if she can shift genders at will, surely she can do anything else she may wish to do.

Like dance.

Sherry Anderson, a spiritual teacher and author, describes a visit by Kwan Yin in which Sherry is coaxed up out of her classic Zen meditative posture to frolic under the trees with this playful bodhisattva. Occurring decades ago, this experience has borne fruit in Sherry's life, manifesting now as an embodied sense of joyful celebration. At the time, Kwan Yin entered an arid situation to wake Sherry up to the Divine Feminine presence she so desperately needed.

Sherry writes:

*As an earnest young Zen student and intensely focused psychologist, I went about finding enlightenment in the same way I did everything else, the only way I knew: driving hard. Pushing. Going for the gold. In the spring of 1976, I embarked on a solo meditation retreat in a tiny cabin in Northern Ontario. From early morning to evening, I did sitting and walking meditations, and 1,000 prostrations a day, when I wasn't chopping wood for the stove.*

# Sandy Boucher

*Really, I was not ready for such an ordeal, having practiced Zen for only a few years. Looking back, I realize how scared I was. Alone for thirty days with nothing but my barely established sitting practice to hold my frantic mind, I seriously thought I might go crazy. I'd heard stories about what could happen if you spent that much time alone. But my Zen master encouraged me and I wanted to give it a try.*

*By around the third day, I'd gotten settled into the retreat structure when something happened that I could never have imagined. As I was sitting erect on my cushion in the afternoon, the sun filtering through the windows, Kwan Yin came into the room and invited me to dance.*

*As I think back, I wonder how I knew she was there. It seemed like the most natural thing. My eyes were open. She was dressed in flowing robes as in the statues I'd seen, and what I remember most was her smile. She looked amused, probably at my plight as a fledgling meditator trying so hard to get it right. She reached out her arms invitingly, as if to say, Come and join me, why don't you? She didn't speak but waited, still smiling, as I struggled to work out what was happening.*

*We're supposed to just sit, I thought. Not get up and dance. I never heard about this sort of thing happening on retreat. Am I doing something wrong?*

*And then she started to move, laughing and sexy and teasing me until there I was, up off my cushion, swaying and whirling and laughing with her. Laughing! Is this what happens on retreat, I wondered. How come nobody told me?*

*Every day she came and every day we danced in the afternoon. I guess I started to expect her, though I can't remember that part any more. But I haven't the slightest difficulty remembering the joy that rose through my body and out my head like a fountain of golden light as great sensual energies whirled me across the room and out the door to turn under the big pines, weeping and laughing, without a scintilla of understanding anything except being there in boundless celebration.*

*I never told my Korean Zen master what happened with Kwan Yin. I think, honestly, I walled off my memory of what happened on that retreat because I had no context for it. Not until twenty years later, when I was writing* The Feminine Face of God *with my friend Pat Hopkins, did I realize: Oh, even then in the midst of what felt like the most severe kind of patriarchal practice, the Sacred Feminine was present. Inviting me to the delicious joy of my feminine self. Filling me with such gladness, releasing my grim and fearful efforting. Inviting me to dance.*

## Hard Times – Memoir and Painting by Eido Frances Carney

Eido Frances Carney is the teacher and resident priest at Olympia Zen Center, Olympia Washington. She is a poet and artist with training in Japan in classic calligraphy techniques. But the following piece draws from an earlier incarnation.

Before she went to Japan and before becoming a Zen priest, Eido was single and raising her family. She was a Zen student and she knew about Kwan Yin who, in the words of the Lotus Sutra, is "the one who can extinguish the woes of existence. . . ." Yet during a grimly unsatisfying and difficult period of her life, Eido lost contact with the bodhisattva in herself. In this piece she tells how she woke up to feel connected once again.

The brush painting accompanying Eido's account of this experience expresses the delight of her new awareness.

Eido writes:

*Living in the cold, windy city of San Francisco, raising three teens, and working a full-time job that sucked the life out of me threw me into a disheartening decline. Every day I would rise early and ride the bus from the fog belt to the financial district to spend the day in front of a computer screen. By the time I trudged home in the evening and walked the six blocks in darkness through driving cold rain, my umbrella turning inside out, I'd be fully spent. Yes, I had meditation, but I began to question its value. Yes, I had notions of Kwan Yin, but where was she?*

*Every day, I teetered on the verge of tears over slight difficulties, and this caused me to be distant from family and friends. I was living with my family, but I began to withdraw. I was quite aware of this condition in myself and found it unnervingly painful. Nevertheless, I couldn't see a clear path to changing my life. Everything came to rock bottom and I could not see the use of my life, nor any future that made sense.*

*One day, I felt unusually depressed. I had to go out to the store and found myself walking up the hill while wondering where I could find solace. Kwan Yin came to mind, but I thought about this being, or spirit, or phantom with a sense of near contempt. I spoke clearly to myself, "All right, I'm sick of this pain, this isolation, this drudgery. If you are real at all, show yourself immediately and give some proof, some help."*

*At that very moment, as I reached the top of the hill, a blind man came around the corner. He heard my footsteps, and simply said, "Good evening!" He said this in an immediate, bright, confirming way, as he tapped his white cane along the street. This man could only hear the world. He could only listen to the sounds around him, and he spoke to what came toward him. "Good evening," I replied, and then he stopped to talk. "I don't know your voice," he said. "Who are you? Do you live on this block?"*

*We chatted for a few moments and, all the while, I knew Kwan Yin had made an appearance. Kwan Yin was not a remote idea but an embodiment of all life around us. As I stood talking to this man, I realized we are all Kwan Yin, in every moment we respond to life with compassion. Sometimes we don't know we are being Kwan Yin, as this man did not, but the timing, the moment, the manifestation rushed through me. A moment earlier, I had demanded proof. Now, here was Kwan Yin before me. Something released in me to soften into greater affection for my children, compassion for my boss and the people I worked with, and a greater capacity to endure the hardships and constraints that go with being the breadwinner. This was the bodhisattva tapping her staff as if to say the sounds of the world everywhere are the everywhere mark of Kwan Yin.*

**Ink Drawing**, Eido Frances Carney

## Compassion for Oneself – Memoir by Genko Rainwater

Genko Rainwater, another Zen priest, recounts the story of her growing awareness of Kwan Yin and the relationship she developed over time, particularly during a painful, confused period of her life. Like Eido Frances Carney, she felt alienated from sources of compassion and power. Following the suggestions of a wise teacher, and watched over by the bodhisattva, she learned to direct compassion to herself, and began to heal.

Her story, while not based on dramatic visions or epiphanies, illustrates the gradual path many of us follow, taking two steps forward and one step back, over years of effort, whether persistent or intermittent, while slowly coming to awareness and acceptance. It's not a colorful or striking path, but incremental and real, the kind of path followed by those of us who tend to plod along rather than leap forward. I count myself a member of this methodical sisterhood. Genko's story resonates within me; other readers may feel the same way.

Genko writes:

*My relationship with Kanzeon/Kwan Yin began several years ago when I was new at Dharma Rain Zen Center in Portland. Every October we do a ceremony that includes chanting the Universal Gateway Chapter of the Lotus Sutra while processing in a serpentine fashion through the zendo. I knew nothing about the Lotus Sutra back then and, as the chant began, I found myself thinking, Yeah, yeah, more hype about how great some deity-or-other is.*

*Oddly enough though, as the litany went on, something sank in. I was listening to the chant describing how Kanzeon will save you from this disaster, Kanzeon will save you from that disaster, call on Kanzeon and she will save you from any disaster, when I began to cry. I was processing, chanting, and crying. I didn't know why, but it was clear there was something here I needed, and I decided to explore this practice further to see if I could find what it was.*

# She Appears!

*Over the next few years, every time we chanted this chapter, I found myself in tears. And I still didn't know why.*

*After some years, as I entered postulancy to become ordained as a Zen priest, I found myself in despair, often fighting feelings of worthlessness. I began to take the chapter's advice to call on Kanzeon. I sat on the side of the zendo where her statue is, and directed my attention to her, feeling her regard for me. I began to use my prayer beads, chanting "Namu Kanzeon Bosatsu" ("I call upon you, Kwan Yin Bodhisattva") 108 times. I found myself stuck in feelings of despair and worthlessness, and found that the chant helped to change my mind state. One night, in particular, I remember paying attention to rising anxiety and despair, just trying to notice and breathe with it, and finally realized I was stuck, I couldn't move past it. So I got out my* mala *to do 108 mantras, just focusing on those for a time. When I had finished, I noticed I was calmer, the anxiety and despair had dissipated, and I could go to sleep peacefully. I speculated that the mantras had interrupted the spiral that had gotten me stuck, and allowed me to let go of those negative emotions and see things more clearly. It didn't change the circumstances, but as I now know, changing the mind changes everything.*

*At some point, my teacher suggested Metta (lovingkindness) practice toward my parents and my young child-self. I put their/our pictures on my altar to do this, and began to feel sick to my stomach. Deciding this practice was too intense for me to do yet, I put the pictures away and began to do the practice for myself alone, sending compassion to myself, calling on Kanzeon for compassion for myself here and now, as a hurting adult. I slowly began to see and trust that I was safe, I could trust Kanzeon to care about me, that I was in a place where no one would attack me for making a mistake. This conscious practice of compassion for myself went on for a couple of years. Eventually, I was able to put a picture of my young child-self back on the altar and practice compassion for her. I got to where I could think of us as friends.*

*In retrospect, I have a sense of what was going on with those tears. The Universal Gateway Chapter of the Lotus Sutra affirms there is a power in the universe that cares. I had just about given up hope for that, and yet deep down I knew it was there, and this is the way things are supposed to be. Something in me knew both the caring and the power existed, and I grieved having lost this knowledge and not knowing how to access it.*

*When I was at my lowest points, I was simply unable to find that power and compassion within myself. I thought if I was having problems, there must be something wrong with me: I was weak, I was fatally flawed. I needed an outside source for compassion (sometimes we call that other-power) in order to believe in it at all.*

*Slowly, over time, with stubborn, consistent practice, I have been gradually able to trust that compassion and power, and to find it in myself so that I can extend it to others.*

## The Nguyen Family – Memoir as told to Sandy Boucher

Because we have been so engaged, as Americans, with the fate of the Vietnamese people, particularly those who took our side during the Vietnam war and had to flee their country when it was over, I am including another of the several accounts I received of Kwan Yin's intervention on behalf of the boat people escaping to the West. (The first was by Lucy Keoni in Chapter Four.)

The following story was sent to me by people who identified themselves only as the Nguyen family. They now live happily in Australia, but theirs was a dangerous journey. It is exemplified in the triumphant sculpture by Miriam Davis that ends this chapter.

The family, including three small children, escaped Vietnam with a group of refugees on a small boat. They well knew the dangers of the trip before them, having heard of the uncertain weather and engine troubles that had stopped other travelers. They particularly feared the pirates who preyed upon boat people, merciless bandits who, after taking everyone's valuables, raped the women, drowned the children, and murdered the men.

Horror of horrors, the family soon realized their boat had been sighted by a pirate vessel, and watched the pirate boat begin to move in their direction. From daylight until sunset on the restless ocean, the pirate boat followed, trying to catch up with the refugee boat, which was sailing at its top speed. Mrs. Nguyen began to call upon Kwan Yin to save them. She chanted and prayed, while the others waited in fear of capture and death. It seemed they would be lost, another group casualty of the war and its aftermath.

But then, with Mrs. Nguyen's chant ringing in their ears, they spied, on the far horizon, the silhouette of an oil rig standing up out of the water like a big black insect.

Mr. Nguyen realized there would surely be foreigners on the rig, and if he and his family could get there first, the pirates would not be able to do their murderous business in full view of these foreign men. During the long anxious day, Mr. Nguyen steered the boat toward the rig. The pirate boat chugged behind trying to catch up, like a lion shadowing its prey, maneuvering to come in for the kill. The Nguyens could see the men with weapons on the distant pirate boat. Mrs. Nguyen prayed to Kwan Yin to keep their engines going strong, and asked the bodhisattva to push their boat toward the oil rig.

The hours passed, and the engine went on laboring, keeping its same distance from the following boat. As night fell, the Nguyen family could see the structure of the rig coming closer and closer, but as darkness came down over them they realized that the workers on the oil rig would not be able to see them. They steered the boat close to the side of the rig and began to circle it, keeping in motion. Mrs. Nguyen once again called upon Kwan Yin to save them.

Through the darkness they could just make out the pirate boat. Would it come close? Would the pirates come aboard and do their brutal work? In darkness, with no help from the men on the rig, who did not know they were there, the Nguyens and the others on the boat suffered the anxiety of not knowing whether they would live through the night.

Finally, in the distance, they heard sounds coming from the pirate boat, commands being given, the slowing of the motor. The pirates had decided not to take the chance of coming closer to the oil rig; they were turning around, going in another direction.

For the rest of the night the Nguyens' boat circled the rig, its passengers at first relieved, then just hoping no new danger would rise up out of the darkness.

It was a joyful morning when the boat people gazed up to see the oil rig workers looking down upon them, and smiling in welcome. The workers shouted encouragement, and sent down treats for the hungry children to eat. Then they gave directions for the boat to go to a nearby landing place in Malaysia, where the people would be taken to a refugee center.

On the Malaysian island where they landed, the Nguyens found their way to a temple dedicated to Kwan Yin. Parents and children entered the temple to offer their profound gratitude to the bodhisattva.

Now, many years later, the Nguyens are sure it was Kwan Yin who saved their lives, showing them the oil rig and guiding them to safety. They continue to thank her for that act and for her beneficent influence toward the prosperous and happy lives they have established in Australia. Every day, Mrs. Nguyen chants the Buddhist sutras and Kwan Yin's name, intoning in Vietnamese, "Namo Quan The Am Bo Tat" ("Hail to you, Kwan Yin Bodhisattva").

## I Hear Your Cries, I Come – Sculpture by Miriam Davis

As if responding directly to the Nguyens' story, artist Miriam Davis created a stirring Kwan Yin. This one has a flamboyant Wonder Woman look as she speeds across the turbulent waters, her arm lifted in a snappy salute, perhaps in response to the steady chanting of Mrs. Nguyen, who believed so strongly in Kwan Yin's power. Who would not be reassured by this image, as she seems to shout, "I hear your cries, I come!"

# She Appears!

**I Hear Your Cries, I Come!**, Miriam Davis

# Chapter Six
## Kwan Yin as Activist

The familiar image of Kwan Yin, beautifully dressed, seated under a willow tree or standing with her vial of precious fluid, radiates equanimity. But she also appears, in some traditional depictions as well as some contemporary ones, brandishing a sword while riding a dragon across a restless ocean. In this embodiment she shows herself as a fierce spirit warrior asking women to inhabit their full brilliance and power. Women activists have taken her warrior spirit with them into social or political conflict zones, or glimpsed her unexpectedly in the midst of scenes of hatred and suspicion.

Kwan Yin wields her sword not to harm or kill, but to cut through confusion, to pierce to the heart of a situation where the truth can be unearthed and where her caring can build bridges between people and douse flames of conflict. She models the fierce compassion that bypasses ineffectual gestures and half-understood agendas to address the hard nub of the problem and open it to solutions. She demands that wisdom be linked to courage, that we step forward to do what we know is right.

Probably all of us have experienced situations in which we realized our kindness and gentleness were either ineffectual or made matters worse: clearly one had to stand firm, to oppose, to refuse, to say "no" or "not this way." This is the fierce compassion Kwan Yin embodies. It can cross and dissolve boundaries; it can disempower hatred. Most of all, this Kwan Yin enters into the full spectrum of life: the chaotic and hurtful, the violent and unfair, as well as the acceptable and civilized parts. In all these aspects of life, she steps forward to support us as we take action to promote justice and alleviate suffering.

I experienced this strongly in 1995 when I attended the United Nations Fourth World Conference on Women in China. On my way there (as I described in Chapter Two), I spent six days on Putuo Shan, Kwan Yin's island, so during my time at the conference, I was filled with an awareness of her. That was fortunate, because before leaving California, I had made a commitment that would place me in jeopardy and call upon my most steadfast belief in human nature.

The UN conference brought together some 26,000 women, social and cultural activists from every country in the world, to address issues such as reproductive rights, poverty, and state and individual violence against women. Women shared strategies for work in these areas, and attended celebrations of women's visions and arts from around the world. In that setting, I experienced Kwan Yin as a general atmosphere, I sensed her in a situation, embodied and expressed by many people. She was Kwan Yin of the thousand arms and thousand eyes.

Preparing for the conference, back in Berkeley, I had attended a session with Tibetan women activists in exile. I vividly remember the scene, which I describe in the first piece in this chapter.

## Standing for Freedom – Memoir by Sandy Boucher

Lhakpa Dolma, a small woman in her forties wearing the *chuba* (brocaded robe) and brightly striped apron that is the traditional costume of Tibet, spoke to us from beneath a photograph of the Dalai Lama. She held her notes with trembling hands, but stepped into her nervousness and rode it, her eyes seeking the gaze of first this woman, and then another.

She told about the mistreatment of Buddhist nuns by the Chinese military, and the forced sterilization of laywomen in Tibet. Then she showed the film, *Satya* or *Prayers for the Enemy* by Ellen Bruno. It presents a chilling depiction of the methods Chinese officials used to subdue Tibetans in their own country. It particularly revealed the courage of the maroon-robed Buddhist nuns who demonstrated against the government and were incarcerated, humiliated, and tortured by the soldiers.

I sat with tears in my eyes, moved both by the message of the film and by Lhakpa's presence. She seemed an embodiment of Kwan Yin, and her willingness to share her story with us made me feel how strongly I was connected to a worldwide community without national or cultural boundaries. In exile, with their men and children, the Tibetan women were building community, maintaining and transmitting their culture, and working peacefully to win back their country. And they were teaching us to pray for our enemies, as the title of the film reminded me. In the truth and enduring gentleness of Lhakpa's expanded view, I recognized the vision of Kwan Yin.

That day in Berkeley, we pledged to do our best to protect the Tibetan women, who were planning to stage a demonstration at the conference in China.

A month later, in Huarou, a town several hours outside Beijing, I stood in the central outdoor area of the non-governmental conference, waiting for the Tibetan women to begin their demonstration. There were less than a dozen of them, so few because the Chinese government had attempted to keep out all immigrant Tibetan women. Lhakpa was not among us, for she had been denied a visa.

Each of us Western women had pledged to stand behind one of the Tibetans, shadowing her to make sure she could not be hustled away by the Chinese plainclothes policemen who watched from the gathering crowd.

Rain lashed the pavement in a relentless, growling torrent. Someone handed me an umbrella to hold over the head of the Tibetan woman before me. The crowd of many thousands huddled in the rain to watch, expectantly, curiously. The secret service men came closer. We waited, and I called upon Kwan Yin, "Please let me be able to meet whatever may happen here. Please let me be as brave as this woman who stands quietly before me."

Then, one of the Tibetan women signaled, and the demonstration began.

Small, delicate, dressed in their traditional garb, the women stepped forward to stand in a line. They took out scarves printed with the Tibetan flag, illegal in China, and tied them over their mouths to symbolize the silencing of the Tibetan people. I moved forward, positioning the umbrella over the woman before me, protecting her back with my body.

There we stood, exposed. The crowd grew quiet as they realized who these women were and what they represented. Everywhere among the curious faces, agents of the Chinese government were taking pictures, making notes, and pushing closer.

Suddenly, I began to tremble. I felt the fragility of these few Tibetan women, so visible here in their defiant gesture. The weight of the billion people who comprised the Chinese nation pressed down upon us; there were so many united against us, and we were so few. It was a crushing sensation, constricting my breath; the umbrella quivered as I struggled to get control of my shaking hands. And then came the awareness that I had felt so strongly on Putuo Shan, on that morning beach only a week before, of Kwan Yin's presence in myself. She was there in the conference courtyard, in this mass of people, some of them hostile to us, and I felt myself expand into my awareness of her. I knew she held us—Chinese, Tibetan, American, every nationality represented here—in her compassionate embrace, connected us to each other in this moment.

The rain drenched my back and continued to pour down from the sky. I held tight to the umbrella handle, looking down at the gleaming black hair and maroon chuba of the woman I was shielding. I knew I would need to stay close to her, for she risked being picked up and made to disappear into a Chinese jail. I hoped it would be all right. I would do my best to protect this woman.

When the demonstration ended, she turned to clasp my hands and thank me. Then she joined her Tibetan sisters huddled under several large umbrellas where they talked quietly together, some blinking back tears. With Kwan Yin's help, they had made their valiant statement.

## Kwan Yin with Loong – Drawing by Alice Sims

Perhaps it was Kwan Yin astride her dragon who came to steady us in China. In this drawing by Alice Sims, the bodhisattva is perfectly at home with her dragon's fierce energy; she's resolute, ardent, yet fully composed. The dragon is a fascinating and common emanation in Chinese culture. This is not the aggressive, warlike creature of our Western imagination, who is most often shown being impaled by St. George's lance. The Chinese "dragon," called a *loong*, is serpent-like, with a long scale-covered body and four legs. Associated with nobility, the loong is thought to have auspicious powers, especially over water, in floods, hurricanes, and monsoons. It is seen as wise and benevolent, symbolizing strength and good luck, and its image is often tattooed on one's body to increase one's power. The loong image adorns clothing, furniture, and buildings. On Chinese New Year, dragon dancers bring it to life on the streets of cities around the world. Many Chinese pray to the image of Kwan Yin riding the dragon, and drivers put such pictures in their cars for protection.

Kwan Yin's ease in mounting and riding such a powerful being came about because she shared her wisdom with the creatures of the ocean depths, and came to protect and rescue them. The King of the

Loongs, who lived in the sea, was so touched by her efforts that he offered himself to be the bodhisattva's steed.

Kwan Yin joins her energy with the loong as a friend or "familiar" who lends her his vast transformative power.

**Kwan Yin with Loong**, Alice Sims

# Two Short Pieces – Stories by Blythe Collier and Susan Nace

In two short pieces, Blythe Collier and Susan Nace tell how Kwan Yin entered their lives and brought a new, empowered perspective.

Blythe, a PhD student in Women's Spirituality at California Institute of Integral Studies, encountered the Kwan Yin of the "royal ease" posture and saw this rendering as the epitome of what a woman can be. As in the coming-to-awareness of seventies feminism, when the guiding perspective was "the personal is political," we could see Blythe's essay as a manifesto of the Second Wave of the Women's Movement, asserting every woman's autonomy as a political statement.

Susan, a classical musician who brings mindful and meditative practices to her teaching, received a small statue of Kwan Yin from a coworker. Caught in a difficult work situation, Susan practiced the quiet activism of simple one-to-one acts of generosity when she called upon Kwan Yin to soften her boss's attitude and transform the situation. Her gesture echoes the methods of nonviolent communication that many activists are adopting to meet political conflict.

Blythe writes:

### Upon First Meeting the Gracious Kwan Yin
*The Lady of Compassion arrived in my life at a time when I was frustratedly, if also unwittingly, looking for a deity on which to model myself: very much a woman, and absolutely unashamed to be so. After all, in my generation I'd been raised with all the classic tropes for nice girls: "girls don't wear pants"; "how are you going to attract a man?"; "sit up straight like a little lady"; "too much jewelry will make you look cheap"; "boys don't like smart girls"; "keep your knees together"; and other phrases of tragic, androcentric nonsense.*

*When I saw the graceful little statuette of the calm, relaxed woman, with one knee up, wearing much lovely jewelry and a beautifully draped skirt, and with her legs unashamedly spread (and, shockingly, I felt absolutely no sense of either shame or titillation in the woman's expression!), I was so relieved on some internal level that, as I stood there and stared, I almost cried. When I saw her smile at me, I felt like I was finally coming home after a long, hard journey in unexpectedly unfriendly lands. To me, Kwan Yin epitomizes what "good girls" really should be: women who are calm and secure in their own beautiful, infinitely varied bodies and selves; women who do not feel a need to either supplicate men for attention, or take responsibility for appeasing any ensuing male violence.*

*For me, Kwan Yin is therefore, and has always been, a place of shelter, both physical and intellectual, and a gentle reminder to practice caring self-love and self-nurturance. She sings to me of comfort and kindness, strength and reassurance; she epitomizes the powerful bonds of friendship between women, of our internal power and brilliance. She is an embodiment of the reality that men are not the center of the universe and women need to be nurtured, as well as to nurture; and she reminds me of my own personal value, intelligence, strength, and beauty, even when I am feeling unsure.*

Susan writes:

### Companion in the Workplace

*Kwan Yin came into my life about seventeen years ago. I admired a statue that was on an engineer's desk where I worked. "She's so beautiful! Who is she?" I asked, "Do you know anything about her?" He replied, "I don't know anything. Someone gave it to me when I left China. Would you like it?" I accepted it, and went on my search to find out who she was.*

*I no longer have that statue, nor several others I have acquired through the years, as she has needed to touch other people's lives and I have given many statues away to those in need.*

*The last time I gave one away, I had been in conflict with my boss at work. We couldn't communicate, we seemed to always misunderstand each other. The conflict became almost unbearable to me, so I made an appointment to see her, and I took with me a statue of Kwan Yin that was on my altar.*

*As I knew it was going to be a difficult conversation, I began with, "I have a gift for you." I held out the statue. "This is Kwan Yin. She's a goddess of compassion, and I want you to know that I have great compassion for you and the challenges of your work."*

*She replied, "Oh, how cute."*

*Somehow, Kwan Yin just didn't seem "cute" to me, but that was where we were.*

*The conversation didn't go very well as I continued with an "I feel" statement, and was reprimanded with a "you don't really feel that." I replied, "Yes, I do feel that way. In fact, I feel very deeply that way."*

*I thought, if anything will get me fired, it will be disagreeing about what I feel!*

*However, I was not fired. I am still at my job and there has been an incredible shift as I've continued to affirm the compassion I have for my boss. Kwan Yin still sits in my boss's office, and I feel she has been the guiding light through some very rocky years. Despite some residual tension, the extreme polarity is gone. I'm hearing more and more a direction of compassion on my boss's part. For this shift, I am profoundly grateful.*

# Kwan Yin with Great Mother Headdress – Carving by Karen Vogel, Drawing of Venus of Laussel by Kirsten Wood

Visual art can make a vivid political statement: its juxtaposition of images can suggest a radical approach to a subject, delivered more strongly than possible through words. In the Buddhist world, it would be challenging to assert that Kwan Yin is not the property of Buddhists, firmly ensconced in their tradition, but reaches back centuries before the Buddha's lifetime (563–483 BCE) to connect to a different lineage. Artist Karen Vogel invites us to contemplate this association in her carved wooden plaque.

Vogel has been creating strong female images for decades. As a feminist artist, rogue scholar, inventive builder, and tarot-card reader in Northern California, she does not hesitate to make surprising connections. With Vicki Noble, she created the Motherpeace Tarot Deck, a groundbreaking goddess-oriented deck of round cards that changed the way women read the Tarot. When she was introduced to Buddhism and Buddhist artwork, she found herself resisting the patriarchal images.

**Kwan Yin with Great Mother Headdress**, Karen Vogel

Traditionally, Kwan Yin's headdress features a seated figure, the Amitabha Buddha, or Buddha of Light, to identify her as belonging to the Buddhist religion. But Karen has chosen to commit a radical political act that, in its imagery, topples traditional Buddhist hierarchy and reliance on the male Buddha figure in favor of the female. She has decorated the headdress with a matriarchal figure much older than the Buddha. The figure is a late Stone Age sculpture from about 22,000 BCE; she is called the Venus of Laussel, though Vogel prefers to call her the Great Mother. Thus, we see Kwan Yin as an emanation of the eternal feminine expressed in her earliest form. The resulting figure bypasses the Buddhist appropriation of Kwan Yin, instead linking her with ancient veneration of the female reproductive body, and suggesting the primacy of women in spiritual life. This is a radical view, challenging long-held assumptions and prejudices.

**Venus of Laussel**, Kirsten Wood

# Dakini Dance – Memoir by Kuya Minogue

Kuya Minogue, a Zen teacher, writer, and social activist, tells of serving as a peacekeeper at a focus group between members of the religious right and the gay community. The Oregon legislature was threatening to enact repressive measures against homosexuals, arousing much emotion on both sides of the issue. A loud, abusive bigot attempted to sabotage the meeting, even threatening Minogue physically. In this very secular, political situation, without warning, and despite her skepticism about deities, Kuya felt herself powerfully embodying Kwan Yin's compassion and directing it to the disruptive person. Something utterly surprising resulted.

Kuya writes:

*As a Zen Buddhist, I've been adamant in my belief that there are no external anthropomorphized deities or bodhisattvas who take a personal interest in my well-being. I've viewed stories about Kwan Yin and the other bodhisattvas as comforting myths. But on the day I'm going to describe, my beliefs were shaken. Kwan Yin was definitely present.*

*It was 1992, an exciting year in US politics; Bill Clinton was campaigning against George W. Bush Senior in a presidential election, and for many gays and lesbians Clinton held out a vision of a kinder, gentler America. But a dark cloud shrouded that vision for gays and lesbians in Oregon, where the Oregon Citizens Alliance, a Christian Right political activist organization, had mounted Ballot Measure 9, which, if approved by voters, would have enshrined the following provisions in the Oregon constitution:*

1. *The state shall not recognize any categorical provision such as sexual identity.*
2. *State, regional, and local governments shall not use resources to support individuals engaging in homosexuality.*

3.  *The education system shall assist in setting a standard that condemns homosexuality as "abnormal, wrong, unnatural and perverse."*

*The measure brought Oregon's gays and lesbians together; we formed a group called, "No-on-9" whose sole purpose was to defeat this ballot measure. I was part of that group. We held rallies, raised money for the campaign, and took to the streets with No-on-9 signs to wave at passing vehicles. In Eugene, Oregon, we met in the house of John, the leader of No-on-9 to design and fold flyers, and to plan our defense strategies.*

*In early October, the fight turned violent: there was a drive-by shooting on a trailer in eastern Oregon and two women were murdered. A lesbian was killed in her apartment in Salem, and a homosexual was beaten nearly to death in a parking lot in Portland. In Eugene, a bomb was thrown at John's house and blew out the front door. Fortunately, it was half an hour after we had finished our meeting and we were socializing at a local bar, so no one was injured or killed. That night, my partner and I awakened in terror when a car passed our home, the Eugene Zen Center, and backfired.*

*Two days after the bombing incident, I received a phone call from Karen, the minister of a local liberal Presbyterian Church, inviting me to represent Buddhism in an interfaith group opposing Ballot Measure 9. Karen and I had co-facilitated a Buddhist/Christian interfaith dialogue called Common Ground in the previous year.*

*"Right now, it looks like all of religion is against homosexuality, and I want to change that," she said.*

*I agreed to meet with her, as well as the Episcopalian chaplain from the University of Oregon, a Catholic priest, a Hindu priest, a Native American spiritual leader, and a Wiccan priestess to plan strategies for a media campaign to counteract the message of the Oregon Citizens Alliance. As part of that group, I helped develop a pamphlet that said on the front cover, "What did Jesus say about homosexuality?" and which, when opened, contained only blank pages. Inspired by King Christian of Denmark's example of inviting all Danes to wear a yellow Jewish star on their clothing during the Nazi invasion, we distributed pink triangles to anyone who would wear them in a Friends of Gays and Lesbians campaign. We held an interfaith service in the Presbyterian Church to affirm our shared belief, as stated in the American Constitution, that "all men are created equal."*

# She Appears!

*After getting some recognition in the media, we decided it was time to meet face to face with members of the Oregon Citizens Alliance who had created Ballot Measure 9, so we planned a focus group and invited both members of the gay and lesbian community and members of the Oregon Citizens Alliance to attend. It was here that Kwan Yin manifested.*

*It was a cool November Saturday when the focus group came together. Sixty-three people, roughly split between members of the gay and lesbian community and adherents of the Christian Right, met in a public conference room on the ground floor of City Hall. It was easy to tell who belonged to which group by the clothes they wore. Gays and lesbians were dressed in jeans and T-shirts; the Christian right were dressed in white shirts, dress pants, skirts, blouses, and sweaters. Because I was a designated peacekeeper, I wore a black band around my left forearm. I had dressed up a little: black jeans, white shirt, black vest, and a red neckerchief. With my crew cut, I looked as one would expect a lesbian to look.*

*We divided the participants into ten small groups of six; where possible, we included three gays or lesbians and three Christian right people in each group. After I gave a short talk on deep listening, and Karen gave a short talk on nonviolent communication, we proposed topics for discussion and gave ten minutes to each topic. "What is your idea of gay/lesbian life?" "What is your idea of the lives of people who adhere to the Christian Right?" "How can we come to a better understanding of each other?" We changed the composition of the groups after each topic.*

*The first two or three rounds started slowly and with a lot of suspicion, but by the third round, the room was buzzing with conversation, and in many cases erupting into laughter. People were beginning to drop long-standing assumptions about each other. I don't know if anyone changed their political position as a result of these talks, but I could see minds opening and changing, body postures relaxing, gestures transforming from pointing and scolding to opening and embracing. Friendships were forming.*

*About halfway into the meeting, a man who had refused to join any group and who had taken up a position alone in the back of the room began to shout out some favorite slogans of the Citizens Alliance. "What's wrong with you people; didn't you read the Bible? It's Adam and Eve, not Adam and Steve!" "Homosexuals are recruiting our children!" "God hates you!"*

*Each time he shouted out a slogan, the conversation would stop briefly while everyone in the room looked up to see who was yelling, and then heads would drop back into the circle, and* conversations would resume. When the participants no longer bothered to look up, the man stood up and took to ranting, mostly about how homosexual teachers were taking over in our schools and more and more children were being recruited every day. As the peacekeeper on his side of the room, I realized it was time to intervene.

I wasn't afraid. I'd been training in Tae Kwon Do for five years and was about to test for a blue belt. I was thin, wiry, fast, and flexible. I could block, feint, and attack in patterns I had practiced so often they were automatic. I knew how to escape 100 variations of grab-and-hold attacks and I could read an opponent's body.

The man was drastically out of shape: a belly hung over his belt, his posture was in a slump, and he had no muscle tone. As I started to move slowly in his direction, I noticed his right hand clench into a fist, so I stopped and turned to attend to the conversation in a nearby group, watching him in my peripheral vision. He relaxed his fist, and once again became absorbed in his rant. I inched my way toward him, planning to invite him to go outside, where I could attempt to talk him down.

When I was about eight yards from him, he turned his invective on me, pointing at me and calling me a sick dyke, a lezzie, an abomination. During his initial rant, his face held a slight smirk, his left lip lifted into a smile of superiority that expressed his belief that he was one with the truth and the rest of us were completely deluded. Occasionally, his eyes lit up with the fervor of fanaticism. But when he realized I was approaching him he snarled, his skin darkened into a dull grey, his eyes flattened, and his jaw clenched so tightly he had to spit his words out through his teeth. When I was about five yards from him, he flared his nostrils, and his eyeballs bulged out. He looked like an enraged, overweight stallion.

For no longer than a flicker of now, a thought arose in my mind. This poor man. What a tremendous suffering his hatred must bring him. Immediately, warmth spread through my body—warmth and love for this man. It began in my throat and then spread into my solar plexus, expanding my heart and penetrating my whole body. I was oozing compassion while holding my intention to debrief the situation.

As this love spread through my body, the man's face and body changed completely. He released his bite so much that his lower jaw hung open. A soft, pink color flowed into his cheeks, his eyes returned to their rightful size and filled with light, and his forehead took on a glow. His body relaxed into a slump, and he looked like a small boy, unconditioned by hatred, open, and receptive. He took two steps backward and fell into his chair. The rant was over.

*I don't think anyone in that room, including myself, really knew what had taken place. As soon as the man sat down, the participants went back to their small group discussions. I moved toward him to invite him outside, but he got up and left. When I went to the door to talk with him, I could see only his back as he waddle-scurried away.*

*I knew Kwan Yin was there. First, she had raised compassion in my heart, and then she had brought a new awareness to the enraged man. I didn't see her, all decked out in her jewels and Chinese court robes, but I suspect the man did. Sometimes I chuckle to think he might have seen me as the Tara form of Kwan Yin, voluptuous, scantily dressed, and doing a dakini dance with scarves and jewels bedecking my dyke body.*

*Whatever he saw, it was compassion that saved us.*

## Kwan Yin with Princess Flowers – Painting by Michele Manning

When tragedy strikes, sometimes there is no way to make the situation better, no activist role open to us. At this point an artist may work simply to honor the event with an imaginative interpretation, to make beauty out of the memory of death and destruction.

On September 11, 2001, our nation reeled before the images of the World Trade Center towers crumbling like cardboard and collapsing into the streets of Manhattan. Artist Michele Manning responded by creating this pastel painting, which depicts her backyard statue of Kwan Yin. While meditating with the statue, Michele noticed the petals of the Princess Flower tree floating around her. She recognized the awful parallel with falling bodies, but called upon Kwan Yin to transform this horror.

She describes her process: "It brought to my mind the most disturbing visual of that terrible day, which was of people jumping from the buildings." But while some would be paralyzed by such a vision, Manning was able to contact a deeper reality. "As I sat there watching the purple petals of the Princess Flower tree fall all around Kwan Yin, I seemed to get a message from her. The petals were the people and she held them all in compassion. She was communicating, *All that is transient is not real and we*

can just let it be. I was then much more peaceful and was inspired to do the pastel of her. It's the only spiritual painting I have done."

The drawing embodies tranquility in the midst of tragedy, but it also suggests we can change our response to events by making something beautiful from their elements, choosing creativity over passivity.

**Kwan Yin with Princess Flowers**, Michele Manning

# Kwan Yin as a Bride in Israel – Memoir and Sculpture by Anita Feng

The longstanding, seemingly unsolvable conflict between Israel and the Palestinian people has displaced thousands and cost countless lives. The cycle of repression and terrorism goes on year after year, until some observers and visitors may feel utterly discouraged that any prospect for peace will prove reliable.

Anita Feng, Zen teacher, writer, and raku ceramic artist, recounts that, while traveling in Israel, she became overwhelmed by the seeming hopelessness of the situation. Yet fresh insight and an unexpected hope awaited her in a chance encounter with a new bride, whose gesture she recognized as Kwan Yin's compassion, and who reminded her that small actions can build bridges between people. Her ceramic bust of the bride brings us into intimate contact with this young Middle Eastern woman.

Anita writes:

*During the second Intifada, in August of 2004, I traveled to the settlements of the West Bank and Gaza Strip, regions of unending conflict and suffering. I undertook this journey in order to complete some research for a novel I had been working on, and as inevitably occurs, I received much more than I bargained for. What ensued was an opportunity to research the front lines of the human heart and mind, and to practice, as my teacher, the late Zen Master Seung Sahn always advised, the interminably wide question: What is this?*

*I traveled with right-wing, ultra-orthodox religious Jews. As much as my political karma was weighted to the left-wing, I found that time spent in a war zone rendered me wingless, filled with a mixture of dread and awe at the suffering so heightened in this part of the world.*

*But early on in my trip, I met Kwan Yin in the guise of a bride who saved, momentarily, the whole world from suffering. It was a moment I will never forget.*

*Our tour group had been bussed to Jaffa, the 6,000-year-old port city just to the south of Tel Aviv. There, we began our walking tour at an ancient stone stairway leading down to the sea. Moshe, the tour guide, told us that it was a popular site for the wedding photographs of brides. On any given day, he explained, there would be brides descending the stairs, each surrounded by their own entourage of photographers.*

*Sure enough, ahead of us were brides with just enough distance between them so as not to inter-fere in each other's photo shoot. With new brides seemingly everywhere, we made an effort to keep out of their way. But as I was stepping past one of them, I was distracted, looking wonderingly at this beautiful woman descending in an impossibly white and glowing gown. I took a step, not looking where. The narrow curved step eluded me and I lost my footing. I would have fallen hard, and might have banged myself up all the way down to the sea and ended my life right there if it were not for the sudden, strong hand of the bride reaching out and grabbing me.*

*At that instant, the whole world smiled. It was as if the photographers, the Arabs, the ultra-orthodox Jews, the tourists, the bride, the sunlight, the stone steps, and the Mediterranean Sea were all part of one large, compassionate mind.*

*I corrected my balance, and tried to stabilize her. After all, she was in her wedding clothes and could have been pulled along with me. It was a risk she had taken without thinking, before thinking. Steeped in the flushed intimacy of that moment, I thanked her. I took her picture, nearly stumbling again as I backed up to frame her face in the viewfinder. Her boldly lined visage smiled with deep patience and kindness. Against a background of ancient and modern walls, her dark, strong shoul-ders glowed in her sleeveless shimmering white dress. She never said a word, and it was unclear if my English or my mumbled words of thanks in Hebrew, "todah raba," were understood. We parted ways. The moment passed.*

*Back in our bullet-proof bus, I overheard two impassioned conversations start up, one in front of me and one behind. It seemed that the little drama of my being saved by a bride provoked some discussion, which revolved around the one topic of whether she was an Arab or a Jew. Dressed in a wedding gown, it was hard to tell. A woman behind me said in a disgruntled tone of voice, "Nowadays, with all kinds of Jews coming to Israel, from Ethiopia, India, Russia, and the Middle East, it's getting harder and harder to tell the difference." Another woman, her eyes narrowed and sharp, said, "Ganze mishpochah," which means "from the other side of the family" in Yiddish, a disparaging remark which meant, in this case, Arab. In front of me, one man, outraged, was saying* to another, "Couldn't have been an Arab. If her husband saw her dressed like that he would have cut off her head before he'd let her go out in public in a sleeveless dress."

I sat in the bus listening, still resonating with the precious quality of being alive in that moment of the bride grabbing hold of my hand, an instant of complete recognition and intimacy. But all of that was already ancient history. The world had since broken into the ten thousand distinctions, and we were back at ground zero: Arab, Jew, right, wrong, correct, and incorrect.

How and when will we meet Kwan Yin again? It behooves us to pay attention; she is, in fact, appearing right now.

**The Bride/Kwan Yin,**
Anita Feng

# The Goddess and the Delivery Man – Memoir by Ava Park

In conservative Orange County of Southern California, there exists a Goddess Temple, presided over by founder and head priestess Ava Park. The temple, formed in 2003, serves Women's Spirituality as the only permanent, physical temple of its kind in the world. A former businesswoman, Ava Park left the corporate sector to focus on her life mission, working with women to restore balance and goodness to the world. She is formally trained in metaphysics and Buddhism, with a degree in Women's Spirituality from the Re-formed Congregation of the Goddess, Inc. The temple, in Irvine, California, often hosts traveling priestesses, and contains a room dedicated to Kwan Yin.

In the following story, Park recounts a troubling incident involving the temple that could have resulted in much suffering, had Kwan Yin not been present.

Ava writes:

*A prominent, internationally known priestess had come from Australia to teach at The Goddess Temple. While leading a daytime chanting class in the main room, she had left her belongings in the adjacent dressing room, including $700 cash in an envelope. Throughout the day, aside from those taking the class, we had had just one visitor to the Temple: a gentleman from a local Asian restaurant who delivered lunch to the Temple for the class. That day, as far as we knew, he had only stayed a moment, just long enough to drop the food off, but we couldn't be sure, as we were all in the back room, with the front door unlocked and the reception area unstaffed.*

*At the end of the class, the priestess discovered to her horror that her money was missing. It was all the money she had made on her teaching tour. Since he was our only visitor, she immediately suspected the restaurant delivery man. Who else could it have been? It would have been so easy for him to slip silently unseen into the dressing room, pocket the cash, and then return to reception to ring the bell and announce himself, as if he'd just arrived.*

# She Appears!

*The visiting priestess asked that we call the establishment and demand the man return immediately to the Temple for questioning.*

*While we were waiting for the suspect to return, the visiting priestess, whose primary goddess is Kwan Yin, prayed to her for truth and a good resolution.*

*A few minutes later, the distraught deliveryman (and, unexpectedly, his employer) presented themselves at our Temple for examination. We all stood awkwardly far apart in the reception area. The delivery man spoke no English and was clearly very upset to be accused of stealing. His hands were shaking; the owner of the restaurant looked furious. I felt the deliveryman was frightened to death of losing his job over this accusation.*

*Standing there uncomfortably, I myself prayed to Kwan Yin for a good resolution. The short priestess approached the tall, thin, forty-something delivery man and stood very close, looking up into his lined and drawn face. "Are you a spiritual man?" she queried. The employer translated the opening question into his worker's native language.*

*The delivery man looked just about ready to weep. Head bowed and humble, he spoke no answer but this: he pulled out from under his shirt the pendant hanging from his neck, a beautiful, jade Kwan Yin, and reverently held the small statue on the golden chain for his challenger to see.*

*The vibration in the room immediately and dramatically changed. Where there had been great tension, fear, and anger, suddenly all was bathed in a beautiful feeling of love and peace. You could literally see the quality of light change in the room around us. Kwan Yin transformed that space and all of us in that moment, and we could all feel it.*

*We broke into smiles, relaxing, and laughing softly. The priestess turned to me with utter certainty: "He didn't do it . . . he didn't do it."*

*We thanked the two men, apologized for the time we had taken, and told them we felt the encounter had been a very specific and synchronous blessing to us all from Kwan Yin herself.*

*The money was never found, but two weeks later, we received a letter from the city police department asking us to be cautious, as there was "a thief operating in the neighborhood," walking into establishments, stealing what he could in a few seconds and leaving quickly, undetected by most. The restaurant delivery man with the goddess around his neck had not, it seemed, been guilty.*

*Of all the thousands of pendant necklaces depicting goddesses, what are the chances that an accused would be wearing the very goddess of his own accuser?*

*Kwan Yin protected an innocent man that day, and blessed us all with truth, and with peaceful, soft hearts.*

*The Temple still orders regularly from that little Asian restaurant. The same delivery man always drops off the order. Now, however, before leaving, he removes his shoes and steps into our Kwan Yin Meditation Room. He bows and gives thanks to his Great Goddess. As he departs, he smiles softly at me.*

*It always seems to me to be the very smile of Kwan Yin herself.*

## Peace Altar – Sculpture by Eleanor Ruckman

Eleanor Ruckman's art incorporates natural materials and discarded manufactured "trash." "As I collect things," she writes, "as I move around outdoors, I hear and see a poignant call for help from the wild world. I share the creative process as a tool for environmental and social justice, safety, health, and peace." She assembled her Peace Altar from materials she found on the sidewalk: a desk drawer, shelf brackets, and a French bread pan.

This combined image was inspired by two sources of the feminine divine: Kwan Yin Bodhisattva, and Our Lady Queen of the Sky, a version of the Virgin Mary said to be "clothed with the sun, and the moon under her feet."

The lotus and meditation posture mark the seated figure as Kwan Yin. The winged dove-heart suggests love; the double spiral at her forehead celebrates the movement from pain and suffering into healing, wholeness, and joy; her hands shape the ancient sign of the *yoni*, or portal, representing feminine sexual and creative energy. She sits inside a *mandorla*, a sacred form suggesting yoni or divine opening, traditionally used for madonnas and in Tibetan art.

Eleanor's Peace Altar is designed not just to express the abiding presence of the bodhisattva: its creation from discarded items and its merging of two sources of transformative female energy constitute a powerful statement in support of our threatened environment, and a call for peace and justice for all beings.

Peace Altar, Eleanor Ruckman

# Kwan Yin's Prayer for the Abuser – Poem by unknown author

I have been unable to find the source of the following prayer. Who could have composed this piercing statement, or who perhaps received it from Kwan Yin herself, in a vision, dream, or meditation? A Zen priest who has been working with this prayer for many years thinks it may come from an ancient Chinese source. But the wording seems to reflect a modern sensibility, and as such has possibly been paraphrased from traditional language into this more accessible form.

The prayer was sent to me by Eddie Buddha Bliss (Eddie Henderson), an Oakland native who is passionate about the safety of children and who is an advocate for their humane treatment. No doubt it inspires him in his activism, expressing a profound wish for the well-being of others, including those who inflict pain and mental suffering.

*To those who withhold refuge,*
*I cradle you in safety at the core of my Being.*
*To those who cause a child to cry out,*
*I grant you the freedom to express your own choked agony.*
*To those who inflict terror,*
*I remind you that you shine with the purity of a thousand suns.*
*To those who would confine, suppress, or deny,*
*I offer the limitless expanse of the sky.*
*To those who need to cut, slash, or burn,*
*I remind you of the invincibility of Spring.*
*To those who cling and grasp,*
*I promise more abundance than you could ever hold onto.*
*To those who vent their rage on small children,*
*I return to you your deepest innocence.*

# She Appears!

*To those who must frighten into submission,*
*I hold you in the bosom of your original mother.*
*To those who cause agony to others,*
*I give the gift of free-flowing tears.*
*To those that deny another's right to be,*
*I remind you that the angels sang in celebration of you on the day of your birth.*
*To those who see only division and separateness,*
*I remind you that a part is born only by bisecting a whole.*
*For those who have forgotten the tender mercy of a mother's embrace,*
*I send a gentle breeze to caress your brow.*
*To those who still feel somehow incomplete,*
*I offer the perfect sanctity of this very moment.*

# Chapter Seven
# Death and Grieving

Almost twenty years have passed since I endured my year of cancer. Now I recall that, as the weeks of chemo took their toll, some of my friends believed I was dying. I looked like someone on her way out; I was skinny and weak, my skin was grayish, and my hair had thinned to wisps. But Kwan Yin kept me steadily focused on the task of staying alive, and through luck, love, and diligence I survived.

During that difficult time, some of the people who were most helpful to me were my illness-buddies in the cancer support group I attended weekly in a nearby church. There I met people who actually were dying, although in a few cases they looked relatively healthy. I found their presence, their stories, and their progress toward death, in which I participated minimally, fascinating and instructive. They were the pro's, who shared sophisticated information about treatments, drugs, and regimens, telling what had worked and what had not worked or made things worse. But I was particularly struck by the dilemma each terminally ill person faced, the dilemma of not-knowing, of always asking themselves: At which particular moment/hour/day should I stop focusing on living as fully as I can, and turn my attention to the dying taking place within me?

I watched and listened to the confusion, sadness, anger, relief, and regret, the whole raw bevy of emotions each person cycled through until they reached their final surrender: Yes I am, now, actually dying. And in that moment, their task changed. Their goal was no longer recovering but letting go, in as physically and psychologically comfortable a situation as could be found. One person stayed angry right to the end, but the others seemed to find a dimension of peace during their final days. Watching this transformation, learning what I could from these examples, I found myself resolving to commit myself more wholeheartedly to every dimension of my life.

This is some of what I know about death. And Kwan Yin's presence, as I wrote in Chapter Three, has been strong in my life ever since. I've discovered that the dying often call upon the bodhisattva to help them make it to "the other side," and to help their survivors deal gently, not only with the dying one but also with themselves. I have seen the calming effect of a simple Kwan Yin altar in the sickroom of a dying friend, and noted the soothing impact of a recorded chant calling upon Kwan Yin during the dying woman's last hours.

The grief that follows death can be deep, powerful, and complex, activating long-dormant feelings and sometimes plunging us into depression. Kwan Yin's presence invites us to turn inward with great kindness, to surround our shaken selves with compassion, to patiently abide with our feelings. The following story concerns not my own death or that of a contemporary, but the sudden death of my brother when I was in my late teens. This event radically altered my life. I spent many years struggling to accept and integrate it. When, later in life, I found Kwan Yin, I encountered a being, an energy, a softening, that could lead me to new understanding of that death.

## What Cannot be Undone – Memoir by Sandy Boucher

My brother George, a stocky, dark-haired, handsome man with a shy smile, shattered his brain with a bullet when he was 28 years old, and disappeared from our lives. His absence exploded in my nineteen-year-old brain, sucking me out into space where I floated alone and desperately lonely for days and months that stretched into years.

It's more than half a century now since we found him dead. I have spent countless hours over those years trying to understand, accept, and mourn his violent exit. For decades, on the anniversary of his death, I felt so sorry that I sobbed. I was sorry George thought he had no other options, and sorry my precious only brother had disappeared, robbing me of knowing him as he aged and changed. My sorrow was anchored in regret that I had not been able to save him, a feeling that has colored my ongoing identification with Kwan Yin in her various manifestations, exploring the domain of compassion and even sacrifice. For decades, I searched for an answer to the question: What could I have done, what sacrifice could I have made to change my brother's circumstances so he would have wanted to go on living?

I tried to understand his action. It is possible George killed himself in part to punish our father, with whom he had struggled all his life and who had, arguably, broken his spirit through constant denigration and occasional physical abuse.

My dad was a carpenter, a big, blunt, outspoken man who was king of our house. He was served the first and largest portion at dinner; he held forth at length while my mother and we children kept silent; and he criticized us children with cold contempt. His conflict with my brother sometimes escalated into violence. Each night at dinner, my father berated George for his dissolute lifestyle. I would watch my brother's head lower in angry shame as Dad called him a loafer, a ne'er do well, a bum. I agreed with my dad that George, in his grease-stained coveralls, often holding a beer and puffing a fat cigar, looked disreputable, and I knew he often acted crudely and carelessly. Yet my father's rants would pierce my heart as I watched the blood rise in George's cheeks and felt his humiliation.

I was the youngest child in my family, and my father's favorite; I identified with him and loved him deeply. When he held me on his lap, his large workman's hands clasped my tummy with warm reassurance. When he lifted me in his arms I knew the world was safe and I was protected. When I pranced around the living room showing off and he laughed at me, I felt showered with grace. My sister and I loved to watch him and my mother, all dressed up like Fred Astaire and Ginger Rogers, twirling across the floor together at the lodge-hall dances. In the kitchen he demonstrated a wacky Charleston for us, his long legs scissoring out to the side, while we choked with laughter.

As I grew up, I came to understand that my dad had wanted to be a doctor, and had even made it through pre-med training at Ohio State University, but his hopes had been destroyed by the Great Depression. The cruel conviction that he had been denied his chance in life ate at him, and he handed the task of realizing his dream to his only son. When George chose to smoke cigars, drink beer, and work on jalopies instead of going to college, my dad vented relentless, frustrated rage upon him.

How could I have made it different? Even in adulthood, this question lingered in my mind, particularly as I began to cultivate a relationship with the Celestial Bodhisattva of Compassion, she who saves people in distress.

I wonder sometimes, would my brother have survived if my mother had acted to protect him? I saw her defend him only once when, after a pushing, shoving match between them, my father lifted my sixteen-year-old brother above his head and, from a landing several steps up the stairway, poised to throw him to the floor. My mother begged my father to put George down, and he did, turning away with trembling arms and a weirdly hangdog look, his fury crumbling into shame.

Given the family dynamics in our home, it seemed I could not have helped my brother and yet, against all reason, for years I found it difficult to forgive myself for not saving George's life. I watched my father abuse him and did not speak. While I could not fully muster the contempt my father wanted us to feel for George, I still did nothing when my father shamed him. When my father labeled him pariah and pushed him outside our family circle, I participated. Even now I wonder how I could have acted to show him he was loved, and whether that would have made a difference. I wonder how I could have sacrificed my own safety and comfort to secure his.

In Kwan Yin lore, there is a famous story about Princess Miao Shan. Because this young girl passionately wanted to pursue a spiritual life and refused to marry the husband chosen by her father, the king, he abused and rejected her. Yet when he became deathly ill, she sacrificed her eyes and hands to save his life. When her father came to thank her, Princess Miao Shan rose into the air, transformed into the thousand-eyed, thousand-armed Kwan Yin. Her father was so affected by her sacrifice and transformation that he changed his ways, learning to practice compassion toward his subjects, and becoming a benevolent ruler of his kingdom instead of the tyrant he had been.

Impressed and troubled by the Miao Shan saga, I plunged back into my own history, to ask my nineteen-year-old self: What could I have sacrificed to save my threatened, vulnerable brother? I was eight years younger than he. I admired him with all my heart and mind and maintained a tender relationship with him when my father was not around. While he sometimes acted the part of the loud, pushy big brother, he was often kind to me, letting me sit next to him on the back step while he contemplated the ancient car he was fixing in the driveway. We would rest in companionable silence, as I sensed the bulk and warmth of his developing male body, so much bigger than mine, and shared the pleasure he took in his car. Sometimes, he would tease me with word-games from the boogie-woogie records he listened to. Sometimes he took me with him on errands, and I would sit proudly erect in the rumble seat of his Model T. It makes me unutterably sad to remember these moments, for it brings home my loss. Each time, I recall that George no longer inhabits this world; he left it long, long ago.

Could Kwan Yin have saved him? What might have happened if I had spoken in his defense? Would my father's rage have turned on me? Would I have sacrificed my favored place as daddy's girl and fallen to the level on the family totem pole that George had sunk to? Would I have been pushed outside the circle of family warmth and approval, as he had been? What if, as I became a teenager myself, I had tried to tell my mother how much my father's treatment of George disturbed me? Would my mother have listened? Would she have joined with me in finding ways to change things?

In our house, no child could raise an objection to anything my dad did; the thought of objecting never even occurred to me. I also understood very early, as I watched my mother support my father in everything, that she would never oppose him.

None of this, however, alters my awareness that young people have been known to defend their siblings, to stand up to authority, even to engage in organized resistance to tyranny and give their very lives. Why not I? Such questions have led me to my fascination with Kwan Yin and the path of compassion.

But Kwan Yin offers us endless opportunities to meet life anew. In my study of her, my reverence for her, my chanting and meditating to contact her, I began to experience a breaking-down of my rigid categories and self-condemnation. I began to feel how helpless my young self had been, and forgive her for her timidity and inaction. Then one day at my cancer support group, I experienced a heart-opening moment that transformed my awareness.

One young man, a Buddhist like me, was dying of prostate cancer. He was a handsome man with dark brown, curly hair and thick-lashed sable eyes. As his condition worsened, he talked about his suffering. At one meeting, I sat next to him and, in my sadness after he had told us of his latest bout with pain and despair, I put my arm around his shoulders. Rather than maintaining a rigidity or distance as some men might have done, he leaned against me and put his head on my shoulder, surrendering to the comfort I offered.

I was inordinately moved, feeling a great rush of tenderness and a sort of relief. It was not until I arrived home that day that I realized it was as if I had been holding and comforting my brother George.

Pondering this experience over the next few days, I remembered the Buddha's response to a woman named Kisagotami who was crazed with grief after the death of her child. She went from house to house in her village, carrying her dead toddler and asking for medicine to make him well. She was turned away, of course, as each householder saw the child was already dead. Finally someone sent her to the Buddha to ask for help. The Buddha saw her plight and promised to bring her child back to life if she would bring him a mustard seed from a house in which no one had died. Her hope renewed, Kisagotami set out again, knocking on doors. But at each house she was told that someone had died there, often more than one person. Defeated, she returned to the Buddha, who asked her "Did you bring me a mustard seed?" Kisagotami responded that she had learned that death happened to everyone, not just her child, and she realized the universal law of the impermanence of all things. After this, she was able to bury the little corpse of her son and take up the life of a spiritual seeker.

The story made me think about all the brothers and sisters who had died throughout all time. It made me recognize my kinship with all the siblings who felt guilty or helpless at their brother's or sister's death. I surrendered to regret, not just for my own situation, but in solidarity with my brother and sister human beings. There must be millions of them throughout the globe, I realized, mourning as I was. I felt Kwan Yin's invitation to welcome all aspects of my humanness, my weakness as well as my strength, my fear as well as my courage. I was no longer alone or lost, but grounded in strong human contact.

In comforting that young man, I had realized that my brother is alive in people who suffer, and while I cannot reach back in time to change his reality, I can aspire to touch him in others, to make myself available to act with delicacy and compassion toward my fellow human beings. I cannot always manage this brave maneuver, but I have Kwan Yin's example before me. And the sense of being held in her compassionate embrace gives me strength.

## Ocean of Compassion – Painting by Lorraine Capparell

In her watercolor of a bodhisattva sitting at the shore, artist Lorraine Capparell evokes the tranquil sense of being surrounded by an endless expanse of fluid. This painting is one in Capparell's "Bodhisattva Series." Remembering my grief for my brother, I am drawn in by this image, comforted by its sense of movement, its reminder of the ever-changing reality of our world of water, earth, and air: the water ebbs and flows but remains the same, while the rocks wear away. The bodhisattva raises her hand in a blessing, as if to acknowledge our grief and hold it in the vast expanse of her understanding.

**Ocean of Compassion**, Lorraine Capparell

# Kwan Yin with Tears – Memoir and Painting by Mary Cutsinger

A wife, a mother, and a widow, artist Mary Cutsinger had a profound connection to Kwan Yin. She was one of the first people to respond to my book, *Discovering Kwan Yin*, when it was published. She sent a passionate, handwritten letter about her life, and photographs of several paintings of Kwan Yin she had made. (I discussed Mary's life in Chapter One, and visited her whimsical side in a painting of hers included in Chapter Five.)

When I knew Mary, she was happily married to her second husband, and her five daughters had become adults. But in that first letter to me, she wrote of a period in her young life when a terrible loss had wracked her existence, and described how a revelation occasioned by Kwan Yin brought her to her necessary grief.

Mary writes:

*I have had numerous spiritual experiences through the years in which Kwan Yin's energy has been present. I was born into a Southern Baptist family, and that in itself almost guarantees a life void of any Buddhist understanding. It is so ironic that my soul made contact with the energy of the Universal Mother of Buddhist roots! Looking back, it all makes perfect sense, but at the time I was perplexed by the experience. The Baptists talked a lot about Jesus and I related to him, very young. But not much time was spent on the female aspect of the godhead, namely Mary, the mother of Jesus. Of course, if I needed a divine mother, to whom would I gravitate? On some level, and God Bless that level of consciousness, I was introduced to the beloved Kwan Yin.*

*I first saw Kwan Yin in the fifties as the magnificent sculpture in the Nelson-Atkins Museum in Kansas City. I was drawn closer to the figure, as if being pulled into a vortex of sacred energy. My thoughts were racing from one question to another. What is this emotion I am feeling? Is this a male or a female? Who is this being? Why does she/he seem to be looking into my soul? Why does she/he look so pleased, so accepting, so at peace with everyone and everything? Is she/he smiling at me? How does she/he know all about me? Why do I feel that she/he feels compassion for me? On and on the questions bombarded my psyche.*

*What am I supposed to do, God? What am I supposed to do with these feelings? I asked. Overwhelmed, I sat down on the floor and started sketching the figure. I had never drawn Asian facial proportions before and it was not easy to do, but I wanted to remember everything about this being, so I drew the whole figure. I felt a deep familiarity with this being. When I looked into the eyes, my own heart felt like it was being hugged. When I looked at the mouth I heard a speaking to an area of my brain, but I could not consciously understand it.*

*But the universe was working to supply my needs. Now when I meditate, I find the energies of Kwan Yin and Mother Mary to be almost the same in softness and compassion. When I first encountered Kwan Yin, little did I know she would guide me through a terrible time.*

*The seventies turned out to be the most challenging period in my entire life. My husband died, and I went into shock. He was only 49 years of age and had no health problems, as far as we knew. So this was a wake-up call for me. Suddenly, I became a 45-year-old widow, mother of five daughters, three of them still young enough to be living at home, and I had major financial problems. In the ten years before my husband died, I had lost my father and my brother to the other side. My husband had lost his mother and his sister. Now, with my husband gone, I was petrified with fear, unable to sleep more than two hours at a time.*

*In one of the art classes I was taking at the college, I was experimenting with the use of an airbrush. I had used the tool for free-hand drawing of a Buddhist head (similar to the image of Kwan Yin). Too much air and too little paint caused the eyelashes to thicken and drip. Thinking I had ruined the painting, I put the image away. That night, in a visionary state, I saw Kwan Yin as that image, and she was crying. The wet eyelashes held tears and there were tears running down her face. When I asked God for an answer to what I had seen, this is the reply I received: "Kwan Yin is crying for you because you are not allowing yourself to grieve." I was trying to be strong for my children and was neglecting my own sorrow. I was trying to be both mother and father, and fathers don't cry. This was a healing for me, as I had no conscious idea of my own feelings. So I began*

allowing myself to grieve.
I painted tears on Kwan
Yin's face in the painting
and to this day I keep
the image hanging in my
art studio to remind me
to remember to nurture
myself. That was 24 years
ago. I am still learning.

Bodhisattva Tears, or,
Kwan Yin with Tears,
**Mary Cutsinger**

# In the Garden – Memoir by Connee Pike

Surely the worst experience for a mother, as illustrated in the Buddhist story of Kisagotami, is the death of a child. Connee Pike tells of a dark time in her life when she lost two babies. Seeking solace, she and her husband found Kwan Yin in the garden behind their house. Kwan Yin offered "a kindness willing to stare into the face of anything, even when everyone else turns away."

Practicing for 25 years in the traditions of the Lakota dream, mystical Christianity, and Tibetan Buddhism, Connee pursued her spiritual work in the world as a hospice chaplain. There she found Kwan Yin to be "a presence teaching me to be present."

In January 2013, with her son in college, Connee moved to an island off the coast of Washington to enter a long-term meditation retreat. "It feels like a natural step in my life," she says. "After years of sitting bedside with the dying, and teaching students, repeatedly I returned to the practices of spiritual presence, a means for being with someone rather than acting upon them. I don't think I had any comprehension of just how vast the practice of presence is. The simplicity fooled me. Now I live in solitude and silence on an island, where I walk, meditate, and write."

Connee writes:

*When I envision Kwan Yin, images of life, not death, arise. And yet we found one another in the corridors of darkness. She was a shining radiance unafraid of the suffering I sought to escape.*

*Years later, when scars replaced open wounds, I became a hospice chaplain, asking as many questions as I answered. I sat at the bedside of the dying seeking the hope that could wrest us all from fear.*

*But what I found was beauty: persistent, ever-present, unyielding.*

*The years before my own initiation had been filled with the dark goddesses, Black Madonna and Kali foremost among them. They flew through my dreams at night while red-tailed hawks and great horned owls hunted nearby. I was a practicing psychotherapist leading women through the labyrinth of domestic violence, incest, rape, and childhood trauma. I understood the necessities of a deity who could scour the countryside to catch trembling souls, destroying everything else along the way.*

*Nevertheless, when death arrived at my door, I was surprised, for I thought myself immune to tragedy. Perhaps this is the case for any healer. We enter into the suffering surrounded by a membrane of helping, believing ourselves protected.*

*My family and I arrived in Oregon to begin our new life. I was pregnant with our second child as we drove into the small rural town we'd call home. We bought a turn-of-the-century house in a neighborhood just shy of the Cascade mountain range, stepping into the dreams we had imagined years before. "We made it," one or the other of us would say as we sat in the breakfast nook with a sketch pad of plans. For me, this meant leaving the world of suffering at the office for a little while, and settling into the nest of family life.*

*But a few weeks after our arrival, I became ill with a lung condition that led to several emergency room visits and difficulties with my pregnancy. Treatment barely abated the symptoms, and as the conditions became more dire I tossed and turned in bed day and night hoping to waylay the threat of early labor, while my three-year-old played with the strangers who soon filled our house with kindness.*

*Roses began to bloom outside the window. I'd watch sparrows pluck bugs from crumbling centers, and listen to starlings screeching from a nearby nest. I'd talk to my unborn baby, implore her really, but everything else was brooding silence, my belly a contemplation upon hope and fear. By summer's end, only seven months pregnant, the bleeding became too severe and labor began. I made the excruciating choice to stop fighting.*

*In the twilight hours, I birthed our daughter, Maggie, who lived and then died an hour later nestled against my naked breast.*

*Eighteen months later, I gave birth to a stillborn son, Oliver. A healthy, full-term baby, he had suffocated dropping into my pelvis for labor, when a knot in the umbilical cord wrapped twice around his neck had tightened, and my breath could no longer reach him.*

*I fell to my knees, broken, asking for the strength to stand up.*

*The mind grasps for familiarity when security slips through the hands. I dug my hands into the soil of a garden that hadn't been tended for thirty years. I needed to grow something.*

*We asked for donations of flower bulbs in Maggie's name and began to cut and pull ivy that blanketed the yard. The property was a tangle of weeds, fallen trees, and forgotten structures. Stone pathways were crumbling. The brick patio ebbed and flowed like earthly waves. We raked leaves, turned hardened dirt, separated out rediscovered toy trinkets, stacked piles of wood and branches, rebuilt a makeshift roof for a shed, inch by inch clearing history for new beginnings.*

*One Saturday morning, we chose to work in a back corner near an outdoor fireplace, thinking enough fall days remained to barbeque. Accustomed to finding treasures, we were careful as we stripped more ivy, when Rob cried, "Look at this."*

*Together we bent over what appeared to be a face, bit by bit unmasking the black stone body. I did not recognize her at first, hair piled atop her head, naked but for a slip of carved silk and jewels, right hand gesturing an unspecified offering. We freed her from all the twines without moving her, for an ominous crack separated her head from her body, though otherwise she displayed only a few scrapes and bruises from her years of sleeping. An interior iron rod could be seen through the opening and together we raised her up and steadied her. She held together.*

*We planted flowers and later Maggie's ashes.*

*Kwan Yin became our patron saint, our keeper of secrets, a witness, a revealed gift surviving against all odds, a reminder that nothing is ever lost. But secretly, I knew she was broken too. And this has made all the difference.*

*I was afraid to leave my prayers with her at first. Having grown up with a god of perfection, I believed that bad things did not happen to good people. I was still trying to be good.*

*But when Oliver died, snow fell upon the whispers of spring and I was too tired to argue anymore. It no longer mattered what prayer is or isn't. I tromped toward her through the garden and for the first time I noticed she was smiling. The Goddess of Compassion, running to the aid of all who suffer, and she smiled. I could not figure out why.*

*Soon after Oliver's death, I began to train as a hospice chaplain.*

*But the first time I saw a fellow human being writhing in pain, death on the horizon, I did not know what to do. Pain medications given, instructions offered, I reached out and took her hand. And waited.*

*She was frail, even before cancer came, born in an era without cheese and meat, her bones light as if to house a bird. But her breath was a torrent through hollowed spaces, her eyes fixed upon mine.*

*We'd never met before, though I knew her story, as she was one of a half-dozen liberals to start a spiritual fellowship based upon equality and social action. Strong, full of conviction, irreverent, and focused, said her friends.*

*We sat together like this for more than an hour communicating across the wires of connection, telling one another our nonverbal stories. I trembled a few times, but she didn't let go of my hand. She didn't clutch for me; rather she held me up, and at first I felt embarrassed because I was supposed to be comforting her. She never blinked or faltered as I learned her rhythms, intuitively understanding I must follow.*

*I could hear a baby crying on the floor above us. The wind stirred outside an open window. The nurses stopped visiting and, alone, we simply sat together.*

*She held her gaze even as the heaviness enveloped all but the continued rising and falling of her breath. I slipped into one of the pauses and joined her journey, forgetting all else but this.*

*On one of the crests of shared space, she smiled. I did too.*

*There was nothing more to do.*

*I would like to say that I have had grand visions of Kwan Yin, tales to resurrect the mysteries, jolt the mind into awakening. But I think that might distort the intimacy. She has been a presence teaching me to be present, a kindness willing to stare into the face of anything, even when everyone else turns away.*

*I have known this loneliness, the self-blame curled around the discomfort of others when grief becomes a valley rather than a bridge. It is as if the lights go out and no one can see anyone else anymore.*

*Kwan Yin didn't rescue me from this place. She greeted me.*

*I spent many hours in the garden sitting before a living statue.*

*There is a freedom in working with the dying that comes from a lack of expectation. The outcome finally decided, we look at one another with fresh eyes. Forgiveness becomes a mirror, not to measure our lives, but to find ourselves within the bigger picture.*

*To be with the dying requires stillness. We cannot be looking for anything. Treasure floats up from within the phenomena we call our lives pointing to a purpose we might have been unable to name before.*

*It's a song really, a scent, a feeling, a presence.*

*I can still remember how Maggie smelled like tulips. The quick pulse of a new shoot pushing through the last dreams of winter. Dirt, melting snow, last year's compost, blood.*

*Not until much later, when I'd sat with hundreds more in these last hours, did I recognize that this was the nature of a soul: ephemeral and perfect.*

*We reveal ourselves in the spaces.*

# She Appears!

*I could not envision Kwan Yin because she never came nor left.*

*Within the liminality of our becoming, we learn to see her.*

*An anthropologist dying of cancer told me, "In the end, we can all agree upon the Great Mother, no matter what name we use."*

*She sought bridges between the Hindu, Catholic, and atheistic tendencies of her family.*

*Tears ran down her face as she began to recite all the names of the Mother she'd heard in her travels around the world.*

*On her last breaths she held a rosary, a gift from her husband passed down several generations of women in his family. Eyes open, she seemed to pause, her breath a palpation instead of movement, as I whispered mantra in Sanskrit, her favorite language of prayer.*

*The sounds floated upon a quiet breeze, a pulse of the way things are.*

*For a moment the beads in her hand vibrated as if turning upon the wheel of her transition. And she leapt, a bubble of water dissolving on a stream.*

*I had not been on pilgrimage yet, but when I did go, I thought of her. She'd told me of her journey to France with questions similar to mine.*

*On the last morning of my trip, I was weak, having been sleepless the night before from the power and sudden purification of spiritual awakening. I sat quietly on the shoreline of the Mediterranean, the sun warming my face as I watched waves dance on a few jutting rocks, when a vision rose upon the water. It seemed to emerge upon an invisible wind, filling the sky to take what I can only call the shape of a woman. I could see the sky through her form as if she lacked solidity, though I could not deny the substance of her existence. Within her womb, I saw every apparition of the Divine Feminine, names rising from the bowels of memory with each transformation. Kwan Yin was among the revelations, clothed with green and magenta silks. She was smiling.*

*Inside the heart of my mind I heard, "I am sorry. I am sorry for all you've been through. To know the heart of the Mother, one must need to be mothered. You cannot embody what you do not know."*

*I had not been forgotten. I had been seen.*

*She is present at every bedside.*

# Kwan Yin and Cosmo – Memoir by Anne Elliott

It is not only human beings whom we love and cherish. Animals can also occupy an important place in our hearts. And when they die, we may experience serious grief. Anne Elliott, a Canadian healer and teacher who facilitates Wheel of the Year Ceremonies honoring the Goddess through the seasons, found herself deeply moved by a small creature who had taken up residence in her house and in her heart.

After years of refusing to allow her family to have a pet, Anne finally opened her door to an animal. She tells of her surprising and sweet time with Cosmo, and how her longtime relationship with Kwan Yin helped her and her family accept his eventual passing.

Anne writes:

*The minute I laid eyes on my first Kwan Yin statue I had a connection with her. Maybe it was because she was the Goddess of Compassion and I had been engaged for many years in compassionate social work supporting women who were adult survivors of childhood sexual abuse. The statue I liked the best was the one where she held a vessel in her left hand, pouring holy water or oil on the earth as a sign of compassion until all suffering ceases. I also like the teaching about Kwan Yin being eligible for Buddhahood, but electing to stay near Earth until there was no more suffering.*

*I began to collect Kwan Yin statues. Every time a family member or friend went abroad, I asked them to bring back a statue. My brother brought a small wooden statue from China, my friend Brian brought a pink glass statue from Malaysia, another friend brought a tall ornate statue from Thailand. I bought a beautiful statue from a gift store in a Buddhist temple outside of Santa Fe and discovered when I got home that it glowed in the dark. How wonderful, I thought. You can be sleeping, wake up, and Kwan Yin will be glowing in the dark for you. Little did I know I was about to have a profound experience of Kwan Yin.*

# She Appears!

*My husband wanted a dog for our family; more specifically, he wanted it for my stepson, who was 14 at the time. Chris had grown up with a dog and he wanted Aaron to have one as well. Having allergies to cats and dogs, I had flatly refused any suggestion of a pet. But after many months of my husband insisting Aaron needed a dog, I agreed to a small, non-shedding breed known as Havanese. The three of us picked him out together and Aaron named him Cosmo.*

*Cosmo, an all-white ball of fluff, became the center of our universe. He was so tiny in those early days that I placed him inside the top of my overalls with his little head peeking out and took him to work (and everywhere else I could). Everyone loved Cosmo, and I couldn't believe, after all my protests about no dogs, how quickly I fell in love with him.*

*After about ten months of our blissful relationship with Cosmo, a friend told me she thought there was something wrong with his eyes. "I've had a lot of dogs over the years," she said, and "I think you need to get Cosmo checked out." Taking her advice, I took him for a checkup. The vet confirmed that there was a problem. "All breeds have a weakness," he said. "In Cosmos's breed, it is the liver. I'll do some tests, but I can tell you right now his liver is enlarged and, given my experience, there is not much I can do."*

*I picked Cosmo up off the examining table, held him close, and said to the vet, "Is he going to die?" "Yes," he said. "How long?" I asked. "Six months, maybe a year," the vet replied.*

*Not being an animal lover prior to Cosmo, I now had to face a new experience, the horrible reality that this little creature I had grown to love was going to leave us. I drove home and went to the master bedroom. I was overcome with sadness. I knew I had to do what I had taught so many others to do: I had to express my feelings. I needed to cry, and to physically feel the emotion stuck in my throat. In seconds, I was crying. As a person who has learned to keep my emotions in, I knew I needed to walk the talk—feel my feelings—as I had said so many times to clients and group participants over the years.*

*I remembered a therapist telling me once that if you decide to take the lid off your emotions and cry hard, your body will stop after about 20 minutes. With this knowledge I allowed myself to weep. Cosmo watched intently as I started to cry; the more I looked at him, the harder I cried. Through my tears and anguish, I kept asking why this had to happen to him, to me, to us.*

*I had never cried so hard in my life. All was wrong with the world, Cosmo would die. I was sobbing so hard the pillow my head was buried in became soaking wet and so did the sheet around the pillow.*

*Then an amazing thing happened. The pillow I had been sobbing into took on a new shape. I immediately stopped crying and watched in utter amazement as a figure formed itself out of the pillow. What is it? I thought. It didn't take long before I realized that the figure was Kwan Yin. With her presence, the room went still, and I stopped crying. I was humbled that the Goddess of Compassion would come to comfort me. I was at peace, and speechless.*

*I shared my encounter with Kwan Yin with my husband and son, and although I don't think they understood my experience completely, they did draw strength from the idea that we need not be afraid of sadness and death.*

*Shortly after this encounter with Kwan Yin, Cosmo was bitten badly in the face by another dog. He was taken immediately to a vet hospital where he spent the night. When he was released the next morning, he was very weak. My husband, son, and I gathered in the living room. My husband held Cosmo on his lap for about 20 minutes, and then gave him to our son to hold for a while. The three of us were very calm, and when my son put Cosmo in my lap, I was filled with gratitude for what he had brought to our family.*

*In about two minutes, my lap was soaked with fluid from Cosmo's body and I knew he had died. Very quietly, I said to my husband and son, "Cosmo has just died." I invited my son to go upstairs and get some sweetgrass incense to burn. The three of us stayed in the silence and stillness with Cosmo till his spirit had left his body. It is hard to say how long we sat together in a circle, but it was a profoundly beautiful time. Cosmo had died with us together as a family. Kwan Yin's holy presence earlier had made it possible for us to accept compassion and to give thanks for the gift of life and death.*

## Meditating Hill – Painting by Lorraine Capparell

Lorraine Capparell offers Kwan Yin's contemplative presence in a painting of hillside, trees, and sky. While in her "Ocean of Compassion" earlier in this chapter, the bodhisattva looked out upon the sea, in this watercolor Kwan Yin is embedded in earth, meditating or sleeping. Kwan Yin, fully present in a wooded hillside, reaching inward to peaceful concentration under a cloudy sky, gives a potent reminder to our grieving selves of our connection to the rhythms of the natural world, the coming-into-existence and the eventual going-out that define the lives and deaths of all beings.

Meditating Hill, **Lorraine Capparell**

# The Wink: A Hospice Story – Memoir by Barbarann Hormann

Marylou Ledwell was an Oakland cabinet-maker whom I met when I was researching *Discovering Kwan Yin*. She told me how much she loved Kwan Yin's playfulness and spontaneity, and how she saw Kwan Yin as a kind of guardian angel. At that time, Marylou was living with incurable lung cancer.

She talked movingly about how Kwan Yin's compassionate presence in her life had allowed her to circumvent a strong tendency implanted in her during her Catholic childhood. Her prayer to Kwan Yin asked, ". . . help me be compassionate to myself, because I have a merciless mind. I have a very strong judge in me." She told me, "That's what Kwan Yin is for me. She helps me remember to be kind to myself."

Kwan Yin brought her to a broader self-acceptance, and as she surrendered to her dying process, she continued to work with the bodhisattva to soften her internal judging and have the best kind of life she could manage while living with lung cancer. "When I'm writing in my journal," she told me, "I will sometimes thank her, sometimes ask her for help. She just feels a lot closer to me, and a lot more accepting, than my old God the Father."

Before the book came out, Marylou died of her cancer, not long after marrying her beloved male companion, Lynn. Her passing, attended by Kwan Yin, family, and many loving friends, was peaceful. Her long, intensely maintained connection with the bodhisattva no doubt contributed to the way she was able to die. The training she had undertaken with Kwan Yin, to bring total acceptance and compassion to herself and others, and to view herself with kindness, helped her in those final days.

Marylou was fortunate to have a friend to aid her in her dying: Barbarann Hormann, a registered nurse and veteran of 25 years doing hospice care. Barbarann is familiar with Kwan Yin and has called upon her in her work with the dying. In the following account, Barbarann gives some vivid details of Marylou's transition, enjoying the playfulness that had characterized Marylou's life and showed itself in a moment near the end.

Barbarann writes:

*On the windowsill of our hospice home stands a Kwan Yin statue. She has helped me in the hard times, in my hospice nursing. I write names on small cards and place them at her feet asking for compassion for patients, family, and friends, and to ask for healing for the suffering I read about daily in the newspapers. Many patients have a difficult time letting go, many families struggle with the death and loss, and Kwan Yin's compassion is there to bring comfort. Often, there is little I can do, but offering people's names to the bodhisattva helps me in my work, as it reminds me that compassion is the heart of hospice.*

*As she was dying of lung cancer, Marylou turned to Kwan Yin for unconditional compassion and acceptance. During her final days and hours at the home of a friend, a statue of Kwan Yin on the bedroom altar watched over her.*

*One evening, her last before her final day of life, friends sat at her bedside reading greetings from the guest book of her wedding. It was then that she truly responded, after hours of no response to voice or touch. I had come to stand at the side of the bed next to our friend Ana, whose home we were all staying in and where Marylou had chosen to spend her last days. Marylou opened her left eye with a clarity and brightness and aliveness I had not seen in the past six hours, and winked directly at Ana with a small smile on her face, a wink that said, "I'm OK and it's all OK." That was the last response experienced by those of us who spent the next eight hours with her, until her death. "OK" was a word Marylou frequently used. She had given friends wooden buttons with "OK" on one side and affirmations on the other side, reminders that "OK" is often good enough.*

*The wink was directed at Ana, but I felt I could claim a little bit of it for myself. After all, it was Marylou who asked me to perform the wedding for her and Lynn the previous day, to marry them in spirit, in love, in a garden filled with family and friends, and with a pure white Kwan Yin statue standing on an altar. Gathering her remaining strength, Marylou went to her wedding in a wheelchair, her Maid of Honor an oxygen tank named Sunshine, decorated with a face, bows, and a garland of flowers. She said her vows loud and clear, and spoke to her family and friends with words for all to remember.*

*The evening of the wink, her physical condition changed rapidly. Two people stayed awake, both to give her medications and support each other in caring for her. We took two-hour shifts, sitting at the bedside, some talking or reading poetry, singing songs, stroking her arm, letting her know that someone was there. Marylou often said she felt supported on a pillow of love, and she left on a pillow of love with her mom and dad, husband and dear friends at her side.*

*An hour before she died, we changed her gown and sheets, removed the oxygen tanks and medical equipment, placed candles and flowers in the room. After her death, we kept her with us for the next twelve hours. The Kwan Yin statue, Goddess of Love and Compassion, stood in the center of the altar in the bedroom. Now, wearing her Japanese robe as the hours went on, she became the purest of white, a white statue of the physical Marylou. Our patients often leave the hospice home within a few hours, so I had not seen what happens to a body in so many hours after death, the relaxing and peace that change the body and the expression.*

*The hospice nurse came, the social worker, friends, and people who just needed to be there. What a healing time it was, what tears were cried, what support for the family and friends to see the peace of death, to have the space and time to reflect. After Marylou's body left, watched over still by the white Kwan Yin, we placed flowers on the made bed, put her picture by the candle, and played some of her favorite music on the tape player. So much better than a stripped bed, an empty room.*

# Kwan Yin and the Star – Painting by Rohmana D'Arezzo

Rohmana D'Arezzo, an internationally recognized artist, is also a Buddhist and astrologer. Her main artistic expression has been the interpretation of goddess archetypes and myths to create a series called "Images of the Sacred Feminine/The Feminine Spirit." In this representation, she depicts Kwan Yin against the night sky, gazing down upon a vast globe of lights, perhaps each one a lighted window in a house where people yearn for liberation from suffering, or mourn the passing of a loved one.

This painting is particularly close to Rohmana's heart, as she painted it shortly after the death of her first-born son, Simon, a week before his 21st birthday. Then, last year, she was struck a terrible blow when her beloved husband died suddenly. The black sky of the painting, and Kwan Yin's downward gaze, take on special meaning to the artist. "It has been unbearable at times," she writes. "My attachment to what was once our life, all gone so suddenly. I see myself in this, grieving, on my knees,

almost draped over her lap."
And she adds, "What else is
there but the Great Mother's
guidance?"

Yet the star in the painting
brings light, and Rohmana
sees it as radiating "brilliant,
universal understanding to
which she is intrinsically
connected, illuminating space
and in turn the world."

**Kwan Yin and the Star**,
Rohmana D'Arezzo

# Remembering Kwan Yin – Memoir by Laura Amazzone

There are few more profound events than the death of one's mother. No matter what the quality of our relationship with her has been, whether we saw her once a year, talked with her daily, or cared for her during her dying process, the death of one's mother awakens one to the truth that "I, too, will die." It can trigger depression, disorientation, and perhaps relief, and may give rise to transformation.

My own mother and I had a distant, unresolved relationship in which five years might go by with only holiday greetings and no visits. Yet when she died, I felt roughly tossed out, all alone, into the universe, and experienced a piercing tenderness for the woman she had been.

Goddess scholar, priestess and author Laura Amazzone endured surprising changes in the wake of her mother's death, developing a different relationship to her sources of strength and safety. Like Connee Pike, she had invoked the fierce Hindu goddesses Kali and Durga, so necessary in her earlier life. Now this no longer felt right. Instead, the bodhisattva arrived, offering a different, gentler inspiration.

Laura writes:

*Since my mother's sudden death two months ago, statues of Kwan Yin keep appearing in front of me in the most unexpected places. Only yesterday, as I sat on a friend's porch marveling at the autumn colors of a northern California mountain forest, it took me about an hour before I noticed a marble Kwan Yin resting on the table in front of me. I was stunned that I had not even seen her or greeted her properly. I had been staring right past her as I enjoyed the vivid patterns of leaves within the trees; I had been reflecting on the effortlessness of these red and yellow leaves falling from the branches that had held and sustained their life until it was time for release. They just let go without struggle, without drama, without fear. Such grace and beauty in their death.*

*Suddenly it dawned on me that maybe this Goddess of Peace and Serenity has been trying to get my attention lately. I remembered several other instances in the past few weeks where Kwan Yin had shown up, but due to my heightened emotional state I had not really taken her in. How is it, I wondered, that it takes me a while before I even notice that she is actually physically there, even when these statues take up a lot of physical space? It is like I look through or past her, and when I finally have become present enough to fully take notice, I am surprised by the calm and accepting look on her face. Although I may have forgotten her, she reminds me that she has never forgotten me.*

*In many respects, this sense of forgetting and being surprised by her unheralded appearance defines my relationship with the gentle, subtle, and yet powerful presence of this Eastern Goddess of Compassion. Most often, when I am struggling and I go to my altar, I cry out to the fierce faces of Kali and Durga, the Divine Mother in her South Asian manifestations, rather than to Kwan Yin. It is not that I doubt Kwan Yin's power, or that I don't remember that she is one of thousands of faces of the same Goddess, but the magnitude of certain life-challenges, especially loss and death, have led me to foolishly believe that only the warrior wisdom aspect of Goddess would be effective in assuaging my fears and sorrow.*

*Yes, fierce goddesses like Kali and Durga have helped me cut through my delusions and heal from certain painful attachments, but lately I have been questioning why I always seem to go into battle to face the intense emotions that arise from life's more formidable experiences. Maybe Kwan Yin keeps appearing to teach me about the strength and answers to be found in stillness and going within? Maybe she is showing me that peace of mind and heart is possible despite the intensity of my emotional struggles. As I try to navigate the complexity and pain of my grief, having lost a mother who had a narcissistic personality and never was able to truly mother me, I see how I have resisted putting down my sword of defense and protection. I have still been fighting the many injustices of our conflicted relationship, even now when there is no more reason to fight. I need more soothing, gentle Kwan-Yin-like ways to face this loss.*

*On Thanksgiving night, I retreated to Harbin Hot Springs in northern California. The place was surprisingly empty and tranquil for a holiday evening. After two months of chaos, pain, and confusion both within and around me since my mother's passing, I was grateful for the peace and near solitude I could experience there. I had come to clear my heart in this sanctuary space, a place I had found refuge in only months earlier after the death of my beloved cat familiar, Gypsy. Missing the rituals around mourning that many cultures honor, I sought out Harbin as a refuge. The Goddess is very present here, as she is at any body of water. Many images of Kwan Yin show her on or near water. Sometimes she carries a pot of healing waters. She helps us with emotional healing and our own spiritual transformation. It felt right to go to these natural spring waters during this time of grieving and seeking connection with mother love. Here in these healing waters, often under the mysterious night sky, I have experienced the serenity and peace of heart and mind I seek. On Thanksgiving, I realized that the soothing energies that comfort me at Harbin are the energies of Kwan Yin.*

*On this particular evening, I made my usual rounds to the steam, sauna, and hot pools, but earlier I had decided I would not go up to the cold pool and do the usual plunge. I was recovering from the flu, and because it was a late November night, it was already cold enough outside. Having felt emotionally uncomfortable for months, I wanted to avoid any more discomfort of any kind, and I do not take well to the cold. But as I soaked in the hot pool, something felt out of balance. I thought about how the light cannot exist without the dark, or life without death. I knew the healing benefits of going from the hot to cold pools, and questioned my resistance to embracing both. Often it is those places of discomfort that bring deep spiritual growth. I knew I at least needed to go up those icy stairs and dip my toes in the cold pool.*

*I made my way to the little pool of ice-cold mountain spring water and, as I reached the deck, I looked to my left and there was Kwan Yin, seated serenely between the trees, three large yellow fig leaves carefully placed in her lap, candles surrounding her and a freshly carved jack o' lantern that spelled out "Give Thanks" to her right. Give thanks for the pain that stretches my heart and for my willingness to surrender to my discomfort and see what transformation awaits. Give thanks for the compassion of the Mother in revealing herself to me in such simple yet beautiful ways. Give thanks for her mercy around my grief of having lost my mother. Give thanks for her gift of liberation from a complicated relationship where much suffering was created and recreated from the roles my mother and I played for each other. Give thanks for the compassion I have for myself, and for my mother. I sat before Kwan Yin on the cold wood bench, praying, praising her, and giving thanks. Under Kwan Yin's protective gaze I could examine my grief, anger, and feelings of abandonment while still feeling gratitude toward my mother for giving me life. I realized that in her death she gave me a gift; she brought me to a path of stillness. She brought me to Kwan Yin.*

*This was not the first time my own mother had connected me to Kwan Yin. Suddenly, I remembered the sweet jade statue of the bodhisattva my mother had given me after her trip to China about a decade ago. Back then we were hardly speaking; maybe this Kwan Yin had come as a reminder of the presence of the peaceful Mother even in the midst of conflict. While I could not speak openly from my heart with my own mother, I could hold this Kwan Yin, who was the size of my hand, and share the contents of my heart. I bowed to the Harbin Kwan Yin for the memories both painful and sweet, the gratitude I was feeling, and the ways my heart was being stretched open, then got up and made my way to the cold pool.*

*I realize that Kwan Yin has been a constant, compassionate, accepting, and comforting presence in my life, so familiar that maybe I took her for granted.*

*When you come into the garden of my red cottage, Kwan Yin greets you. Her face is serene despite the chips all over her orange-brown concrete body. Her body, weathered and worn, reminds me of how my own body has felt having spent decades fighting illness and healing from family abuse and deep-seated traumas. This rust-colored Kwan Yin has been with me for over a decade. In fact, Kwan Yin was the very first goddess statue I received as a gift. I reflect on how she sat by me through my divorce, the loss of two cats, the death of one of my best friends, and most recently, the death of my mother. She stood by me while I went to graduate school and held down a full-time teaching job. After numerous trips to India and Nepal, she was always there to greet me upon my return. She has witnessed the fears and excitement that have come from changing jobs, moving from northern to southern California, and writing and publishing a book. She has held me as I have fallen in and out of love. Once, when I was transporting her to a ritual, a glass bottle I was holding flew out of my hand and crashed into her head, decapitating her. I was stunned by the Kali-esque symbolism of this "accident" and glued her head back on. Kwan Yin has picked me up when I have been broken; I did the same for her.*

*These days, I am experiencing the strength that comes from calmness and serenity. Once again, Kwan Yin guides me through one of the fiercer of life's experiences—death and grief—and I am taking notice. I allow myself to open to a compassionate, merciful, loving mother instead of always being ready for warrior mode. Being in this space, I know and see Kwan Yin has been with me longer than I was acknowledging or even fully accepting. She has always been there guiding and waiting to hold me. Her qualities of compassion, mercy, peace, and tranquility have always been available to me. She is not loud, nor is she a warrior, but she is there, strong, centered, and composed, showing me a new approach to healing my suffering and experiencing transformation and liberation. And she has been with me for longer than I know.*

# Chapter Eight
## Final Words

Why does it matter that you and I care so much about Kwan Yin? Why do we need her example, her arrival in our lives, her guidance and wisdom? Looking around me I see a world in crisis mode. I watch the gradual destruction of our precious earth: the melting of the ice caps, the rising of the waters, the degradation of whole environments in which animals and birds are struggling to survive. I receive constant news of violent death, displacement of whole populations to become refugees, rape and trafficking of women and children. I live with the fact that, in this United States, the richest country in the world, children and their parents go hungry every day, people struggle to access the healthcare and other services they need, and certain groups find themselves in prison for the profit of others. Whom can I call upon?

Kwan Yin turns toward it all, offering us, as Connee Pike wrote, "a kindness willing to stare into the face of anything, even when everyone else turns away." The bodhisattva models a way to be here, fully, in whatever mode we find ourselves. She announces her presence in a hundred ways. Some are dramatic, like the efforts of doctors and aid workers who risk their lives to sustain the desperate people caught in war zones, or like the fireperson or pilot whose expertise and sangfroid save the lives of many. But, more familiarly in my life, she has shown herself in the gestures of kind, ordinary people I see every day: the clerk in the grocery store who helps me with my bags, the driver who waves me ahead in thick rush-hour traffic, the friend who notices when I'm struggling and calls me up, and in myself when I stop, look, realize what is needed.

Florence Caplow put it succinctly: "I suspect that the great forces of compassion of the world, personified as Mother Mary or Kwan Yin, do not actually come when we call them; they're here all the time, hidden, waiting with a deep and inexhaustible patience for us. They're hidden all around us, and also within us. It is up to us to notice . . ." So Kwan Yin is here, as I sit at my computer writing these words, she's here in this very body and mind, in this very situation.

It's up to us to keep her presence in mind as we meet the challenges of our suffering world. It's up to us, in any situation, to stop, fully inhabit our own Kwan Yin nature, see what must be done, and do it. Her compassion is changing our world daily. May we participate with her in every moment, that we may live with clarity and courage.

And may we always remember to be kind to ourselves when it's time to take a break.

**Kwan Yin Takes a Break**,
Miriam Davis

# Acknowledgements

My gratitude goes to the writers and artists whose work appears in the preceding pages. I thank them not only for trusting me with their powerful and beautiful work, but also for their patience and timely responses to my editing and questions. I also thank the people who sent articles and artwork that did not become part of this book, as difficult as those choices often were.

Two women were with me from the beginning: Vicki Noble, female shaman, author, healer, and ritualist, who sent out my first tentative appeal for material on Kwan Yin to her wonderfully responsive mailing list; and my friend Nonnie Welch, artist and owner of Spirit Matters store, with whom I have shared many in-depth conversations, over many years, about the Bodhisattva of Compassion. I also offer my appreciation to Professor Chung-Fang Yu, who knows more about Kwan Yin than anyone.

To Sandy Butler, Nan Gefen, Barbara Gates, Kirsten Wood, and Joni Anderson, who read the book in manuscript and offered excellent feedback, and to Sam Dennison and Kirsten Wood, who both provided technical assistance, I offer many thanks.

Carol Newhouse and Annie Hershey have cheered me on from the start. Their Women's Dharma Foundation helped facilitate my fund drive; and Moonifest Foundation awarded me a most welcome grant. To Annabelle Zinsser, for her generous support of my work, I offer my enduring gratitude. And I heartily thank the many friends who helped provide the opportunity for me to give my time to this book's coming together: Martha Boesing, Nan Gefen, Jen Biehn and Joan Lohman, Carolyn Burwell, Ruth Denison, Sheila Khalov, Heidi Thompson, Chuck Pliske, Sandy Butler, Kitty Costello, Darlene Fung and Boann Perry, Edie Hartshorne, Marilyn Sewell, Lynda Koolish, Judith Ragir, Cappy Coates and Veronica Selver, Chellis Glendinning, Michele Manning, Lew Carson and Suzanne Savage.

To my publishers Anne Key and Candace Kant, of Goddess Ink Publishing Company, thank you so much for your enthusiasm and support.

And to my life-partner, Martha Boesing, who is my confidante, my moral support, and my most stringent critic: You sat with me for all those hours helping to sort out and put in order the multitude of materials I received. You read and re-read four drafts of this book, and offered insightful responses and useful suggestions throughout. My gratitude is deep and wide.

# About the Contributors

**Laura Amazzone**, MA, is an author, teacher, priestess, and intuitive. Her book, *Goddess Durga and Sacred Female Power*, won the 2011 Enheduanna award for Excellence in Women-centered literature. Laura teaches classes and workshops. She lives near the ocean in Venice, California. www.lauraamazzone.com

**Sherry Ruth Anderson** lives in California with her husband, Paul Ray. She is a writer and teaches the Diamond Approach to Spiritual Development® in the US and Holland. Her latest book is *Ripening Time: Inside Stories for Aging with Grace*. www.sherryruthanderson.com

**Paula Arai**, Harvard PhD in Buddhist Studies, is the author of *Women Living Zen: Japanese Buddhist Nuns* (Oxford University Press) and *Bringing Zen Home: The Healing Heart of Japanese Women's Rituals* (University of Hawaii Press). She teaches at Louisiana State University.

**Meredith Balgley**: "I have lived half of my life in the mountains of Asheville, North Carolina, with my husband where we homebirthed and homeschooled our wonderful two sons. There has always been a lot of travel, music, dance, and adventure." merbalgley@hotmail.com

**Pamala Bird**, sculptor, printmaker, mother, grandmother, and retired graphic designer, lives in southern Utah, and holds a Bachelor of Fine Arts degree from Utah State University. Creating bas relief sculptures honoring feminine archetypes has been personally empowering for her. www.PamBirdArt.com

**Doti Boon**: "Mother of two, grandmother of seven and, at 75, engaged to my partner of 30 years. I am founder and pastor of Center for Creative Living, a spiritual/metaphysical community. I offer psychic readings into a person's future, present, and past." centerforcreativeliving-ucm.com

**Lesanne Brooke** lives in Somerset West, Cape Town, South Africa, with "my long-time love, our two children, a dog, a cat, and a gerbil." She is a shaman, writer, and executive coach facilitating corporate change processes and leadership development. @blissdragon (Twitter) and blissdragon.blogspot.com

**Reena Burton** grew up in a renovated farmhouse near Sebastopol, California. Oak trees, mud pies, sisterhood, bare feet, and bonfires are among the elements that shaped her childhood spirit. Service, ritual, community, and Women's Spirituality have helped to develop her adult creative sight. www.reenaburton.com

**Zenshin Florence Caplow** is a Soto Zen priest, dharma teacher, field botanist, essayist, and editor. Her most recent book, with Susan Moon, is *The Hidden Lamp: Stories from Twenty-Five Centuries of Awakened Women*. Her essays can be read on Slipping Glimpser. zenshin-edz.blogspot.ca

**Lorraine Capparell** has been recognized for her work as a painter, sculptor, and photographer since 1975. She studied at Cornell and San Francisco State University, and has traveled widely in Asia to study art. Her work can be seen on her website, skymuseum.com

**Eido Frances Carney** is founder and abbess of Olympia Zen Center. She received Dharma Transmission from Niho Tetsumei Roshi in lineage with Ryokan. She is a poet, painter, and author of *Kakurenbo or the Whereabouts of Zen Priest Ryokan*. olympiazencenter.org/

**Nancy Cavaretta**, PhD, is a faculty member in Special Education at Roosevelt University in Chicago, specializing in early childhood autism. She researches full inclusion and its impact on teacher retention. She is the mother of three grown children. ncavaret@roosevelt.edu

**Elaine Chan-Scherer**, San Francisco psychotherapist and artist, creates images that represent and inspire connection with the Sacred Feminine. She lives with her husband Karl in their newly empty nest, enjoying the flight patterns of their beloved daughters. artsfelaine@gmail.com

# She Appears!

**Blythe** "Collie" Collier is a Bay Area writer and doctoral student at the California Institute of Integral Studies Women's Spirituality program, living with her "undomesticated partner" of 25 years. She is well-traveled, loves modern matrifocal cultures, and is plotting to overthrow the current dominant paradigm. She asks: "ANY QUESTIONS?!" ColliesBestiary.com

**Mary Cutsinger** was born in 1931 in Oklahoma, and lived her last years in Ridgecrest, California. Besides raising five children, Mary produced an accomplished body of work in pastel, oil, and water-color. She died in 2008, having influenced many both spiritually and artistically.

**Rohmana D'Arezzo's** work spans four decades. Images of the Sacred Feminine/The Feminine Spirit have been her main expression through interpretations of goddess archetypes and myths. In 1998, she created *manacraft goddess arts*. She is a Buddhist practitioner and an astrologer. goddessarts.com

**Max Dashu** is an artist, writer, videographer, and teacher of global women's history and heritages. She does online courses and webcasts, and publishes posters and DVDs, most recently *Woman Shaman: the Ancients*. She lives in Oakland, California. www.suppressedhistories.net

**Miriam Davis** is a studio artist living on the northern California coast. She has been showing her work nationally since 1987 and has taught ceramic sculpture, painting, and mixed media for more than fifteen years. She has a husband and one daughter. miriamdavis.com

**Shoshanah Dubiner** lived in San Francisco for fifty years before moving to Ashland, Oregon in 2004. She lives with her husband. Her artistic career spans costume, stage, graphic design, museum exhibition design, painting, and drawing. www.cybermuse.com.

**Anne Elliot**, Purple Goddess, is a healer/teacher who hosts goddess-inspired wheel-of-the-year ceremonies and leads Divine Feminine pilgrimages. Co-author of an upcoming book on wheel-of-the-year rituals, Anne lives in Sorrento, British Columbia, with her husband Christopher. amelliott@telus.net

**Laura Fargas** is a Washington, DC, poet, and mostly retired attorney who has published one book of poems, *An Animal of the Sixth Day*. Emerging from ten years of rather severe illness, she hopes to find a publisher for her second book.

**Anita Feng** works as a writer and sculptor specializing in raku ceramic Buddhas and Kwan Yins. She teaches Zen in Seattle, Washington, and lives with her family in nearby Issaquah. Her sculptures and books can be seen at www.Golden-Wind.com

**Jacqueline Gautier** is a Registered Clinical Counselor in British Columbia, Canada. She lives in Nanaimo, on Vancouver Island, where, besides enjoying her private practice and consulting, she hikes, does yoga, and plays tennis. www.jacquelinegautier.com

**Diane Musho Hamilton** is executive director and co-founder, with her husband Michael Mugaku Zimmerman, of Two Arrows Zen, a center for Zen study and practice in Utah. Diane is the author of *Everything is Workable: A Zen Approach to Conflict Resolution.* www.dianemushohamilton.com

**Francene Hart** is a visionary artist whose work hangs in collections of healers and seekers around the planet. She is artist and author of the Sacred Geometry Oracle Deck and Sacred Geometry Cards for the Visionary Path. www.francenehart.com and francene@francenehart.com

**Barbarann Hormann** is a Registered Nurse who worked for 25 years at Nancy Hinds Hospice in Fresno, California. She retired in June, 2013. She has been married for 42 years to John Hormann, and is a soft sculpture artist.

**Fred Kahn** grew up in a multicultural family: Russian-Jewish, Mexican-Native American. His grandparents were members of the Theosophical Society. He has done radio theater and off-Broadway storytelling. Fred currently works at Walmart and is a professional storyteller, as well as a Tibetan Buddhist.

**Mary B. Kelly**, artist, professor of art and author, has taught at many institutions and exhibited her paintings widely. She lives near the ocean on Hilton Head, South Carolina. www.marykellystudio.homestead.com and kellym13@juno.com

**Lucy Keoni** is a happiness coach, dreamcatcher, transformation catalyst, human rights activist, and lover of life who is native to northern California. livelaughluvlearn.tumblr.com

# She Appears!

**Marilyn Lastra-McGinley**, married to Charles, has three adult children and four grandchildren. She grew up in Union City, New Jersey, and is currently living in Rutherford, NJ. Marilyn worked for many years as an administrative assistant and enjoys being a stay-at-home grandmother.

**Yvonne MacKenzie** was born in Scotland, emigrating to Canada in the sixties. She lives on Pender Island, British Columbia, with her cat Rumi and son Morgan. Her poetry book is titled *Stillpoint*, and she is currently working on a collection of short stories. heartwoodsong@gmail.com

**Margaret Mann** is a writer, counselor, and art museum docent in Honolulu, Hawaii, and happily single. She is the author of *A Dramatically Different Direction*, which deals with surviving a serious disability. www.adramaticallydifferentdirection.com

**Michèle Manning** enjoyed her career for 25 years as illustrator and fine artist in the San Francisco Bay Area. Her artwork still hangs in the Strawberry Creek Design Studio building, Berkeley, where she had a studio. She is now blissfully retired in Maui. www.michelemanning.com

**Kuya Minogue** lives with her partner in Creston, British Columbia. She is resident teacher at the Creston Zendo, where she teaches Zen practice and Zen Writing Practice. She is founder of the Kootenay Centre for Mindfulness. www.zenwords.ca

**Musawa** calls herself a "deep lez eco-feminist, earth-and-goddess-loving womyn from way back." She taught Women's Studies and started We'Moon Land community in the early seventies, founded We'Moon (the datebook) in the early eighties, and became a Hakomi mind-body therapist in the nineties. www.wemoon.ws

**Susan Nace** is a classical musician, teacher, and coach. She brought mindfulness to her school through Chade Meng Tan's Search Inside Yourself program. Susan practices meditation and Tai Chi and, since 1985, incorporates mindful and meditative practices in her teaching.

**Willow B. Norris** lives and works on Maui, Hawaii. A significant portion of her work features Kwan Yin and Buddha. Her paintings, prints, and cards can be seen and purchased on her website. www.willowbnorris.com

**Rev. Ava Park** is the Founder/Presiding Priestess of The Goddess Temple of Orange County, a 3,200-square-foot permanent temple in Irvine, California. Ava is also the originator of The Queen Teachings ™ for women, and author of *Queen of Your Realm*. www.GoddessTempleOC.org

**Connee L. Pike**, MS, is the author of *Song to the Dakini* and *Standing on the Edge of Magic*. When her son, Zach, left for college, she moved to an island off the coast of Washington to write and meditate. www.conneepike.com

**Ursula Popp** is an eclectic healer-medicine woman and educator. Born in Switzerland, she now lives in Seattle with her dog, Sam. Her writing can be found in professional journals, *The Sun* magazine, and *Secret Histories: Stories of Courage, Risk, and Revelation*. www.ursulapopp.com

**Genko Rainwater** is a full-time Soto Zen priest serving Dharma Rain Zen Center in Portland, Oregon. In addition to her siblings, two sons, and four grandchildren, she finds that "the sangha is my family, whom I live with and rely on." www.dharma-rain.org

**Estrella Root** recently joined a local Zen sangha in Santa Fe. She has communicated, revered, and related to a number of goddesses, including Kwan Yin, in her over forty years as a "medium priestess (not a high one)" in the Wiccan Way.

**Eleanor Ruckman** is a Registered Art Therapist and licensed Marriage and Family Therapist, living and practicing in the California Bay Area. Making art, for her, is a spiritual practice and a tool for social and environmental justice. www.ArtGivesHope.com

**Lydia Ruyle**, artist, author, scholar emerita of the Visual Arts faculty of the University of Northern Colorado, began to create her Goddess Icon Spirit Banners in 1995. Her family consists of a husband of 56 years, three children and their spouses, and six grandchildren. www.lydiaruyle.com and lydiaruyle@aol.com

**Marcia Anissa Schenkel** works as a substitute teacher in Madison, Wisconsin. She paints buddhas, bodhisattvas, and micro/macrocosmic abstracts, and digitally creates and prints mandalas, as well as sewing large and small hangings of devotional images. treehugger1@tds.net

# She Appears!

**Alice Sims**, an artist, is married and has two children, who are both artists. For over ten years, she has been president of Art for the People, a nonprofit that brings art to low-income people. www.artforthepeople.org

**Kimberly Eve (Jaia) Snyder** is a much-published illustrator through Ash Tree Publishing, Woodstock, New York, and is currently working on a children's book called *Welcome Weeds!* She also expresses her artistic medicine through face painting. www.kimberlyeve.com and www.capecodfacepainter.com

**Maya Telford**, after many years of working with textile art, has returned to painting on canvas, often depicting the Divine Feminine. A Canadian, she combines her spiritual work and painting with teaching, with a heavy emphasis on the sacred feminine. www.mayatelford.com and maya@mayatelford.com

**Karen Vogel**, Tarot reader, artist, rogue scholar, and inventive builder, was trained in anthropology and art. Her work includes Motherpeace Tarot Deck (with Vicki Noble), *Motherpeace Tarot Guidebook*, and *Coyote Tails*. She lives in Occidental, California with her partner, Lisa, and Willow, their cat. www.karenvogelstudio.com

**Kate Lila Wheeler** is finishing the writing of her second novel, *Holy Woman*, between teaching Buddhist meditation retreats. She lives in Somerville, Massachusetts, with her husband, David M. Guss, an anthropologist, professor, and poet. www.katewheeler.com

**Gayle M. Wilde** is a native of Washington, and lives in Olympia. She has two grown children and one grandchild. Her career background is in behavioral health, and she is currently a shamanistic practitioner in the Celtic tradition. www.heartsourcejourneys.com

**Kirsten Wood** is a lifelong devotee of the Divine Mother in her many diverse forms, who loves creating music and art. She is honored to be included in this beautiful presentation of Kwan Yin and the courageous women who have generously offered their stories here.

# About the Author

Sandy Boucher, MA, is a Buddhist author, editor, and teacher who has been active for 35 years in the San Francisco Bay Area and Pacific Northwest. She is author of *Turning the Wheel: American Women Creating the New Buddhism*, a groundbreaking exploration of women's participation in Buddhist practice. Her other Dharma books include *Discovering Kwan Yin: Buddhist Goddess of Compassion*, *Hidden Spring: A Buddhist Woman Confronts Cancer*, *Dancing in the Dharma: The Life and Teachings of Ruth Denison*, and *Opening the Lotus: A Woman's Guide to Buddhism*.

In 2006, she was selected by an international committee of scholars and practitioners as an Outstanding Woman in Buddhism at the United Nations headquarters in Bangkok; and has received a National Endowment for the Arts Fellowship in Literature. She leads retreats on Dharma and Writing, co-leads the Meditation and the Spirit of Creativity retreat at Spirit Rock Meditation Center in California, and, with her life-partner Martha Boesing, leads the New Year's Women's Retreat at Great Vow Zen Center in Oregon.

Sandy lives in Oakland, California with her partner, and feels held in their family of three children, spouses, and grandchildren.

**Other books by Goddess Ink:**

*Heart of the Sun: An Anthology in Exaltation of Sekhmet*
edited by Candace Kant and Anne Key

*Desert Priestess: a memoir*
by Anne Key

*Brigit: Sun of Womanhood*
edited by Patricia Monaghan and Michael McDermott

*Stepping Into Ourselves: An Anthology of Writings on Priestesses*
edited by Anne Key and Candace Kant

Goddess Ink
*books for the heart and mind*
www.goddess-ink.com

CPSIA information can be obtained
at www.ICGtesting.com
Printed in the USA
LVHW070716301121
704790LV00004B/11